MW01036835

"COME, LORD JESUS"

—Rev. 22.20

"Come, Lord Jesus"

A Study of the Book of Revelation

WATCHMAN NEE

Christian Fellowship Publishers, Inc.
New York

Copyright © 1976
Christian Fellowship Publishers, Inc.
New York
All Rights Reserved
ISBN 0-935008-16-0

Available from the Publishers at:

11515 Allecingie Parkway
Richmond, Virginia 23235

Printed in the United States of America

TRANSLATOR'S PREFACE

This study was given by Mr. Watchman Nee in the early years of his ministry. Longhand notes which provided the gist of these readings were taken at the time. They were copied and mimeographed but never published in book form. In the study of prophecy our brother followed the approach of such people as G. H. Pember, Robert Govett and D. M. Panton, though he no doubt had his own original views and interpretations. As one can never be dogmatic in prophetic study, our brother merely presented here what seemed to help and satisfy him most. His purpose was to provoke the interest of God's people on prophecy and to prepare them in meeting the blessed Lord.

As his own spiritual life became more matured, he later on took a more spiritual approach to the book of Revelation, without, however, overturning his former basic understanding. In this connection, then, the reader will notice that the translator has attempted to include in the various translator's notes whatever important improvements our brother had made in his own interpretations.

Further, the reader should also be aware that in the original Chinese longhand notes, mentioned above, that part of the study dealing with Revelation 2.19–3.22 was found missing. For the sake of completion, the translator has endeavored to fill in the gap by translating and using the pertinent portion of Mr. Nee's later work which was entitled *Church Orthodoxy*.

CONTENTS

Scripture quotations are from the
American Standard Version of the Bible
(1901), unless otherwise indicated.

PART ONE

THE VISION OF THE GLORIOUS LORD

The Vision of the Glorious Lord
(1.1-20)

This section draws attention to several things; namely, (1) the meaning of this revelation, (2) the procedure by which this revelation is given, and (3) the significance of this revelation.

(1) The meaning of this revelation. "The Revelation of Jesus Christ"—There is a difference between revelation and inspiration. Revelation is the unveiling of God to men in order to make them see; inspiration is the leading of God within men. The phrase "the Revelation of Jesus Christ" has a dual meaning: (a) it is Jesus Christ himself who unveils the things which must shortly come to pass, and these are the things that are recorded in this book; and (b) this book also reveals Jesus Christ himself—it discloses how He will overcome, receive glory, and become King.

(2) The procedure by which this revelation is given. (a) "God gave him Christ"—Herein are we shown the order in the universe. God is the highest of all: "All things are of God" (2 Cor. 5.18). We are also shown that even though the Lord has ascended to heaven He yet keeps His place as a bond-servant. As He was on earth, so is He in heaven (see John 5.19,20; 12.49,50; Mark 13.32). Not because He is now in glory does He refuse to keep His place. How very different He is from the archangel (Ez. 38.11-19).

(b) "And he sent and signified it by his angel"—

Most of the writings of the Scriptures come through the hands of the angels (Acts 7.38; Heb. 2.2); for the angels are ministering spirits (Heb. 1.14).

(c) "Signified . . . unto his servant John"—"signified" means to point out or to perform.

(d) "Who bare witness of the word of God, and of the testimony of Jesus Christ, even of all things that he saw"—John records the revelation he has received and delivers it to us. What he delivers is the word of God and the testimony of Jesus Christ.

(3) The significance of this revelation. (a) "The things which must shortly come to pass"—"Must" means not subject to any change. "Shortly come" speaks of that which is not to be delayed. Yet we are just too neglectful and too procrastinating about these things. (b) "To show unto his servants"—This revelation is not concerned with a few people; rather, it relates to all the servants. The word "servants" is "bond-servants" in the original. We all are the bond-slaves of the Lord because we have been bought by Him with His blood (1 Cor. 6.20). (c) Here is a promise: "Blessed is he that readeth, and they that hear the words of the prophecy, and keep the things that are written therein" (v. 3). The same promise is given in 22.7, though there is no more mention of "read" and "hear"; for as we reach the time of chapter 22, all have read and heard; hence the primary thing in view there is to "keep".

"For the time is at hand"—"The time" is that of the second coming of the Lord. A time which touches many aspects (11.15–18). Here, though, it refers primarily to the blessings believers will receive. Since the time is at hand, why do we not see it arriving now? It is due to the fact of the long-suffering of the Lord towards the world (2 Peter 3.8,9). Yet also, it is because the believers are not yet ready. Consequently, the time is still to come. Nevertheless, the conditions of the world as well as of the church at our day reassure us that the time is at hand.

1.4–5a SALUTATION AND BLESSING

"John to the seven churches that are in Asia"—Although each of the seven churches receives its own letter, at the same time John sends the whole book to all seven churches in Asia. "Seven" is a perfect number. The seven churches represent all the churches. Therefore, the message is for us as well.

The words of salutation resemble those used by Paul: "Grace to you and peace". But the name of the triune God is different here from that in the other New Testament epistles: (a) "From him who is and who was and who is to come"—This is God's name. He is the same yesterday, today, and forever. The world is soon to undergo a drastic change, but God never changes. For this reason, grace and peace change not; (b) "And from the seven Spirits that are before his throne"—The "seven Spirits" does not mean that there are seven Spirits (Eph. 4); it merely indicates the manifold works of the one Holy Spirit (Rev. 4.5; 5.6); (c) "And from Jesus Christ, who is the faithful witness, the firstborn of the dead, and the ruler of the kings of the earth"—This speaks of the work which the Lord has done on earth, how He has overcome, and what glory He will have in the future. We have such a triune God to grant us grace and peace.

1.5b–7 DOXOLOGY

As John arrives at this juncture in his writing, he cannot help but burst forth in praise. He praises for two reasons: "Unto him that loveth us"—The love of Christ is two-fold:

(a) the past—"And loosed us from our sins by his blood",
and (b) the present and future experience—"And he made
us to be a kingdom, to be priests unto his God and Father":
what we now experience will be fully realized in the future.
And as we ourselves think of this, we will truly say with
John: "To him be the glory and the dominion for ever and
ever. Amen."

When John thinks upon the love which he has received,
how can he refrain from praises? Yet in the meantime he
envisages the situation of the world at the return of Christ,
and so he gives a word of warning in verse 7. "Behold" is a
word to call our attention to what is going to be proclaimed.
"He cometh with the cloud"—Just as He went up to heaven
with a cloud, so shall He come back with the cloud. The
word here is in perfect accord with what is said in Acts 1.9–
11. Then: "And every eye shall see him, and they that
pierced him; and all the tribes of the earth shall mourn over
him. Even so, Amen"—These words agree with Matthew
24.30.

1.8 THE TESTIMONY OF GOD

Here God bears witness concerning himself that He is
the One who is the same, and He is the Almighty One. The
purpose of such a declaration is to encourage us to wholly
trust Him in time of tribulation.

1.9–10a JOHN'S NARRATIVE OF HIS OWN CURRENT SITUATION

(1) Concerning himself. "I John, your brother and
partaker with you in the tribulation and kingdom and
patience"—Although John has seen such tremendous visions, he still calls himself our brother. How humble he is!
At that time he is in tribulation, but he also mentions

the kingdom; for through many tribulations must we enter the kingdom (cf. Acts 14.22). Since we have the hope of the kingdom, we must therefore be patient. So then, this patience has in it the meaning of patiently waiting for the kingdom. "Partaker with you" indicates that the kingdom is the portion of all. Hence all must share as well in tribulation and patience.

(2) His environment. "I . . . was in the isle called Patmos, for the word of God and the testimony of Jesus"— He was at that time being persecuted for the sake of God's word and was exiled to an island. Though he was lonely, being shut in from all sides, the Lord was nonetheless with him, the door to heaven was wide open towards him, and he received new revelation. For this reason, tribulation is our great blessing.

(3) The day on which John saw the vision was the Lord's day, that is to say, the first day of the seven-day week. Some suggest that it was the day of the Lord, which is the day of Jehovah.*

(4) The spirit of the visioner. "I was in the Spirit"— Though John suffered much in the body, his spirit was strong and active.

1.10b–16 THE VISION OF THE GLORIOUS CHRIST

(1) The voice heard was a great voice as of a trumpet. A trumpet is sounded to gather people together. Here the Lord was especially calling John to write to the seven churches. These seven churches actually existed at the time. They were specially chosen to serve as types of the church throughout the ages.

(2) The sight seen was the seven golden candlesticks (or

---

* But this is unlikely.—*Translator*

lampstands), which are the seven churches (v.20). Such are the churches in God's view, which ought to be their spiritual reality, since the churches are to illuminate this dark world for the Lord. Yet the candlesticks themselves cannot give out light unless they are filled with oil. And hence the churches need to be filled with the Holy Spirit.

(3) "One like unto a son of man"—The Son of man was in the midst of the candlesticks to inspect the churches (2.1). What was the likeness of this Man? He looked like a son of man, which is to imply that He was somewhat different from what He had been on earth. So the word "like" is used. As to His appearance, it was described as follows:

(a) "Clothed with a garment down to the foot"—which signifies the Lord's glory, the glory that He had before His incarnation (Is. 6.1). He is now being restored to His former glory. The garment not only signifies His original glory, it also indicates His priesthood; for He is now our high priest (Heb. 8.1).

(b) "And girt about at the breasts with a golden girdle"—which attests to His righteousness and faithfulness (Is. 11.5).

(c) "And his head and his hair were white as white wool, white as snow"—which shows how He is in possession of glory (Prov. 16.31, 20.29) and holiness (Dan. 7.9).

(d) "And his eyes were as a flame of fire"—which fire is used for proving (1 Peter 1.7) so that whatever is good or bad may be manifested. With His eyes as a flame of fire everything will be exposed immediately by His look. The fire referred to in 1 Corinthians 3.13 is the fire of the Lord's eyes. The meaning of 1 Corinthians 4.5 likewise agrees with what is expressed here.

(e) "And his feet like unto burnished brass"—feet are for walking and brass in the Bible typifies judgment. Wherever the brazen feet go, there goes judgment. Since the

Lord's feet are now in the church, the Lord is presently judging His church first (1 Peter 4.17).

(f) "And his voice as the voice of many waters"—which denotes that His voice is full of majesty and power (Ps. 29.4).

(g) "And he had in his right hand seven stars"—which stars are the angels (or messengers) of the seven churches (v.20). Their being in the Lord's hand means that they are being used, controlled, and protected by the Lord.

(h) "And out of his mouth proceeded a sharp two-edged sword"—which sword is used to deal with the world as well as with the church (19.15–21, 2.16).

(i) "And his countenance was as the sun shineth in his strength"—the Lord was manifested in the same way on the mount of transfiguration (Matt. 17.2). The scene on the mount of transfiguration typifies the kingdom, because the Lord is most glorious in the kingdom.

1.17–20 THE LORD'S COMMISSION

Each time the Lord appears to man, it is accompanied by His commission. And this time is not any different from the other times. "And when I saw him, I fell at his feet as one dead"—The glory of Christ is such that when John saw it he became as one dead. This was not only true of John, it was likewise true of Isaiah (6.1–5), of Job (42.5,6) and of Daniel (10.2–9).

John was not only a saved person but also one who had been most intimate with the Lord; and yet, when he saw the Lord of Glory he fell as one dead. What, then, would happen to the unsaved or carnal person if he should see the Lord? Hence the Scriptures make clear that the man of flesh cannot inherit the kingdom of God (Gal. 5.19–21) nor can the unregenerated ever see it (John 3.3). How meaningful this is! A carnal or unclean person is truly unfit to see the Lord of Glory. Indeed, when Christ shall come in the future His glory will be even greater than that of today; no wonder many will faint for fear and cry to the mountains to hide them (Rev. 6.16; Luke 21.26).

"And he laid his right hand upon me, saying, Fear not"—How merciful! Though He is in glory, His love has not diminished. If the future glory were not mingled with love we would not be able to be benefited much by it. The hand that on earth once touched many a sick person touches still; the word which once comforted many a broken-hearted one yet speaks. His hand and His word not only comforted John but also gave strength (cf. Dan. 8.17,18; 10.9,10,18,19). Hand to give strength and word by which to feel comforted. When John realized that the Lord's love remained the same as before, fear naturally left him and strength and comfort became his portion instead.

"I am the first . . . the keys of death and of Hades"— Here we find that the Lord used two ways to reveal himself:

(1) with His glory. As soon as John saw it, he knew.

(2) with His word. This pertains to what is inward, that which John could not see with his physical eyes. Hence the Lord also had to use words to unveil himself. From what He said we can gather three things about Him.

(a) His position. "I am the first and the last"—This is the title of Jehovah found in the Old Testament (Is. 41.4, 44.6, 48.12). It distinguishes Him as the God who changes not.

(b) His life. "And the Living one; and I was dead, and behold, I am alive for evermore"—This shows that He has the eternal life. Though He once died for the sins of men, yet now is He resurrected; and He will die no more, since He ever lives.

(c) His authority. "And I have the keys of death and

of Hades"—Let us look closely at this point. "Death" is related to the physical body, whereas "Hades" is related to the soul. Immediately after one dies, his soul enters Hades. Hades means the nether regions, located at the center of the earth (Matt. 12.40; Num. 16.30–33). Hades is divided into two compartments: one is the place of torture for the unsaved, the other is the place of rest for the saved (Luke 16.19–31). Yet such a division is temporary because *eternal* separation exists between the new heaven and the new earth on the one hand and the lake of fire on the other. "Keys" are used to open doors, thus indicating that both death and Hades have doors which may be closed (Matt. 16.18; Acts 2.24). Whoever *holds* these keys likewise has the authority. Formerly the power of death and Hades was in Satan's hand (Heb. 2.14; Matt. 16.18), but since the Lord was raised from the dead, Hades and death have lost their power, and the keys to them are now delivered into the Lord's hand. Oh, what a victory this is! For this reason, the Lord is able at the millennial kingdom to release freely those who belong to Him.

"Write therefore the things which thou sawest, and the things which are, and the things which shall come to pass hereafter"—The meaning of "therefore" is to continue on with what has been said already. Because of the victory of the Lord, "therefore" these things ought to be written.

Moreover, this verse lays clearly before us the division of this book: (1) the things seen (the past), (2) the things which are (the present), and (3) the things which shall come to pass hereafter (the future). The word "sawest" in the original is in perfect form, which indicates that something has already been seen. This refers to the vision which John saw as recorded in chapter 1. The things which are mean the things which are now existing, and hence these are the things that exist during the church age as reported in chapters 2 and 3. The things which shall come to pass hereafter are those things that will continue to happen after the church age. All the chapters after chapter 4 up to chapter 19 are the descriptions of these things which are to come.

"The mystery of the seven stars which thou sawest in my right hand and the seven golden candlesticks. The seven stars are the angels of the seven churches: and the seven candlesticks are seven churches"—Even though the book of Revelation contains a large number of mysteries, they become clear revelations as these mysteries are explained by the book itself. The candlesticks are the churches; this is easily acknowledged. And the seven stars are the seven angels. But *who* are these angels? Some commentators explain that the angels refer to pastors or bishops. If this is so, then what do the churches themselves refer to, since their angels refer to something else? If the churches are churches, then the angels should simply be angels too. Furthermore, the angels themselves are the interpretation of the mystery of the stars. If we were to explain the angels in this manner as referring to pastors or bishops we would be interpreting mystery by means of mystery. We are fairly certain that the Lord does not intend it that way. What, therefore, should we say regarding the angels? The most plausible answer is: these angels are angels, just as the churches are churches.

Yet what *kind* of angels are they? For according to the Scriptures there are two kinds: angels in heaven (Matt. 22.30) and human messengers (Hag. 1.13). The angels here cannot point to those in heaven because (a) the angels in heaven, though they may minister to the church, are unable to bear responsibility of the church; (b) the angels in heaven are spiritual beings, and thus they cannot receive physical letters; (c) inasmuch as this book is signified to

John by the Lord through His angel, how can the angel write about himself? and (d) the Lord calls upon the angel in Smyrna to be faithful unto death (2.10), but this is something impossible for an angel in heaven to experience.

Since, then, these are not angels in heaven, they must be human messengers. The Bible supplies us with examples, such as in 2 Corinthians 8.23 and Philippians 2.25. A further point which we need to notice here is the fact that messengers are representatives. They are able to represent the churches. Thus they are symbolized in the form of stars before the Lord, for stars give light; therefore they show forth the spiritual conditions of the various churches. And finally, the stars being in the Lord's hand signifies that they are being used by Him and are thus given authority.

PART TWO

THE SEVEN CHURCHES

The Seven Churches
(2.1–3.22)

(1) Seven different churches—The seven churches in these two chapters are churches which actually existed at that time, and the situations described were also the actual conditions of these various churches. Yet, these seven churches in addition represent seven periods in church history along with their respective characteristics. However, these characteristics are not absolutely or exclusively applicable to each period; it is only that, for example, the post-apostolic church has a resemblance more to Ephesus, that the second generation church is more like Smyrna, and so forth. But as a matter of fact the post-apostolic church has the conditions of the other six churches as well.

(2) The seven angels—Each letter is addressed to an angel. We have already discussed who these angels are. May the Lord raise us up as messengers. Although every letter is written to the angel, it is nonetheless given to the church. Hence it concerns every believer.

(3) Seven self-styled addresses—In each letter our Lord utters something of himself, and what He says fits perfectly as the remedy to the condition of each church. For instance, Ephesus is a church which has lost its first love, so the Lord reveals himself as one who walks in the midst of the golden candlesticks. Smyrna being a suffering church, to her the Lord manifests himself as the one who was dead and lives

again so as to encourage them to be martyrs. Pergamum is a worldly church, hence the Lord unveils himself as the one with the sharp two-edged sword able to cut the world asunder. Thyatira is a corrupted adulterous church, therefore the Lord appears with eyes as a flame of fire and feet like burnished brass in order to inspect and to judge. Sardis is a dead church, consequently the Lord shows himself forth as the one who has the Spirit of life (the seven Spirits of God) and the shining stars. Philadelphia is a church faithfully keeping the truth, and so the Lord proclaims himself as He who is holy and true and who opens wide to them the door of labor. Laodicea is a church full of human opinions, and for this reason the Lord discloses that He is the Head over all creation.

(4) Meaning of the seven localities—Ephesus means "desire" or "loosening", which shows how they have left their first love. The word Smyrna comes from the word myrrh, which means "bitter", thus signifying that period when the church suffered under the Roman persecutions. Pergamum signifies "high tower", thus representing the church with worldly power and position after the Roman Emperor Constantine the Great accepted Christianity. Thyatira denotes "sacrificing untiringly", which description fits well the period of the rise of the Catholic system with the instigation of the special priesthood and of idol-worship. This may be considered the darkest and most corrupted age of the church. As to its meaning, Sardis connotes "revival" or "restoration"—a development which happened at the time of the Reformation, with nonetheless its spiritual condition still weak or dead. Philadelphia speaks of "brotherly love", which had its exemplification over a hundred years ago when there was such a recovery of the church that some Christians left all sects behind, joined together in love, and kept faithfully the truths in the Bible. Laodicea

suggests "people's opinions", and how this applies appropriately to the condition of the church today that is so full of men's opinions.

(5) Seven "I know" 's—Each letter includes the words "I know". The Lord knows our conduct, whether good or bad. He does His best to commend the good, but He also severely reprimands the bad. This is the token of the righteous judgment of the Lord.

(6) Seven exhortations—Each church has its own peculiar situation, and the Lord exhorts each of them accordingly. His words of exhortation to the various churches are recorded in Revelation 2 and 3 as follows: to Ephesus (2.4,5), to Smyrna (2.10), to Pergamum (2.14–16), to Thyatira (2.20–25), to Sardis (3.2,3), to Philadelphia (3.11), and to Laodicea (3.17–20).

(7) Seven promises—The Lord raises up overcomers in each church for the purpose of maintaining His testimony. To them He gives special promises. These promises are given in 2.7, 2.10–11, 2.17, 2.26–28, 3.5, 3.12, and 3.21.

(8) Seven calls—Each letter contains the words "He that hath an ear, let him hear what the Spirit saith to the churches" (2.7, 2.11, 2.29, 3.6, 3.13, and 3.22). Since these seven letters are dictated by the Lord himself, why does the record read that it is the Holy Spirit who speaks to the churches? In spite of the fact that the Lord speaks directly to John, the churches can only read what John has written. So that in the reading of them, there must be the enlightening of the Holy Spirit in order to understand. Furthermore, even when the Lord was on earth, He never spoke by himself but always spoke by the Holy Spirit. Today He still speaks by the Holy Spirit. Accordingly, it is the same as the Holy Spirit speaking to the churches.

Let us now take a closer look at the contents of each letter.

2.1-7 THE CHURCH IN EPHESUS

2.1 "Write"—John serves as the Lord's secretary. He is to record what the Lord has said.

"The church in Ephesus"—The church has two different aspects: one is the mystic church, the other is the local church. One is the body of Christ, the other is the house of God. The churches referred to in these two chapters are the churches in each locality. Great is the distinction between "the church *in* Ephesus" and "the church *of* Ephesus", for the church only *sojourns* at Ephesus, it does not *belong* to Ephesus. For this reason, names such as the Roman Catholic Church, the Greek Orthodox Church, the Chinese Church, and so forth are unscriptural.

"To the angel"—This letter to Ephesus is addressed to the messenger. How very different is this from Paul's letter to the Ephesians. There Paul wrote to all the believers, whereas here, due to the departures from earthly life or declensions in spiritual life, only the messenger was able to receive this letter. A comparison of the two letters will further reveal the great difference in that church's situation then and now. Ephesus has indeed "loosened" itself, has drawn back, and been damaged.

The Lord shows forth himself to this church as the one "that holdeth the seven stars in his right hand, he that walketh in the midst of the seven golden candlesticks" so as to cause the church in Ephesus and its messenger to know that He possesses full authority and examines all His churches.

2.2,3 These are words of commendation by the Lord.

What He commends touches three perspectives. (1) Regarding themselves: (a) Works—they must have had good works; (b) Toil—they must have labored diligently; and (c) Patience—they had the parent's heart so as to bear and forbear the weaknesses of other people. (2) Regarding the management of the church: (a) They do not bear evil men (cf. 1 Cor. 5); and (b) They do not accept workers carelessly—nay, they even test the apostles. All this shows that they have spiritual discernment. (3) Regarding the world: They patiently bear for the Lord's name and do not grow weary. From this description we might conclude that the church in Ephesus is most perfect.

2.4 Though the church in Ephesus looks so good, the Lord nevertheless has something against her; she has lost her first love. We may wonder how a truly working church can be so lacking in inward love towards the Lord. Yet experience tells us that there may be outside activities even though the first love within is already lost. The "first love" is the best and most perfect love.

The question may be raised, How is the first love lost? (1) It may be due to an over-emphasis on works rather than on loving the Lord. (2) It may be due to disobedience to the Lord (John 15.10).

Herein are we shown that what the Lord requires is our love towards Him. If there are toil and spiritual knowledge and yet there is no love, all is useless (1 Thess. 1.2,3; 1 Cor. 13.2).

2.5 The Lord tells them a way of restoration. (1) "Remember therefore whence thou art fallen"—This means there should be an investigation of the cause. There is a reason for each retrogression. Unless the cause is found, restoration is impossible. According to the Lord's view, even though the church in Ephesus is outwardly perfect she has already fallen inwardly. Inner fall precedes outer failure. (2) "And repent"—Repentance is not only required of sinners, it is likewise necessary for believers. Whenever there is a falling away, there is the need for repentance. (3) "And do the first works"—Repentance is negative, while "do the first works" is positive.

From this word we may deduce that the church in Ephesus is not doing what she really did before. What were the things that she previously did? We know these could not have been toil, patience, diligence, resisting evil men, and so forth. In spite of the fact that nothing is explicitly mentioned, a careful reading of the letter to the Ephesians will convince us of two things which they had been doing before: (1) they were faithful (1.1), and (2) they let Christ be Lord (3.17). Hence, in this verse the Lord shows the way to restoration on the one hand and discloses His judgment on the other—the way of first love, but then followed by a warning: "Or else I come to thee, and will move thy candlestick out of its place, except thou repent"—Move the candlestick out of its place! Since the word candlestick represents the church, the duty of the church is to shine, that is, to witness.

To be removed from its place is a word that prompts us to ask what *is* the church's place. The original place of all these candlesticks is before the Lord (1.12,13; 2.1). And hence, to be removed from its place will mean that a given church will lose its original place before the Lord and thus be rejected by Him. Having lost its place, the candlestick is no longer supplied with oil (that is to say, the church can no longer be filled with the Holy Spirit), and consequently it is unable to shine for the Lord. The point in view here is not concerned with salvation, rather is it a matter of work and testimony. There are many churches today that are simply removed candlesticks in the eyes of the Lord.

2.6 "Nicolaitans" means, in the original, "those who conquer the people"; this then refers to a party that lusts after power and takes upon itself the position of leadership. The Lord hates the works of these people. He commends the Ephesian believers because they are able to hate what He hates.

2.7 "He that hath an ear, let him hear what the Spirit saith to the churches"—Such a refrain shows that this letter is given not only to the church in Ephesus but also to all the churches which may be in a situation similar to that of the church in Ephesus. Alas, how few are those who will hear the Lord's words, although they are indeed addressed to all the churches. "He that hath an ear" connotes the sad fact of how many there are in the church who have no ear to hear.

Why is there no ear to hear the Lord's words? This does not refer to the physical but to the spiritual ear. This can be easily understood by reading Matthew 13.13–15. Why do some people not have any spiritual ear? Because (1) they have no spiritual aspiration, and (2) they are in fact afraid of the Lord's word.

Finally, reward is mentioned. "To him that overcometh"—Here the word "him" is singular in number. In spite of the fact that the church as a whole has failed, individuals may still seek after victory. What the Lord seeks in these seven letters is for people to overcome.

The reward which the overcomers will receive is that they shall eat of the tree of life which is in the Paradise of God. This paradise or garden most likely points to the one in the kingdom of the heavens, because the kingdom of the heavens is to restore the condition of Genesis 2. As there was on earth a garden of Eden as recorded in Genesis 2, so there will be a paradise in the kingdom of the heavens. What joy the overcomer will have in being with the Lord in Paradise! And not just a being in Paradise, but able also to eat the fruit of the tree of life.

2.8-11 THE CHURCH IN SMYRNA

The church in Smyrna represents the condition of the church from the second century up to the year 313 after Christ.

The church in Ephesus is cold as to her love, whereas the church in Smyrna suffers greatly. This is most meaningful, since the Lord frequently uses suffering to revive believers who have turned cold or have become loose.

2.8 The word Smyrna signifies "bitterness" which comes from the root word "myrrh"—Myrrh is most precious; and hence this suffering is a precious suffering. All who suffer for the Lord are truly precious.

"The first and the last" denotes that the Lord is the God who changes not. What comfort this Name gives to the church in Smyrna.

"Who was dead, and lived again"—These were the experiences of our Lord while on earth. It gives great consolation and encouragement and help to the believers in Smyrna: (1) The Lord leaves with us an example. If He had to die while on earth, can we be spared? (2) Since He suffered unto death, He is well able to sympathize with us (Heb. 4.15). (3) In order to accomplish God's purpose and overcome the enemy, He must suffer death; likewise, we need to suffer that we too may succeed. (4) Though He died, yet He lives again. There is hope, and it will not be in vain if we suffer or die for the Lord.

2.9 "I know"—(1) The Lord knows all about our sufferings. Our hearts should therefore rest. (2) Since He knows our sufferings but still does not take them away from us, it can only mean that such sufferings are profitable to us. (3) Knowing our sufferings now, He undoubtedly knows how to reward us in the future.

The sufferings which the church in Smyrna endures are three-fold: (1) tribulation, (2) poverty, and (3) blasphemy.

(1) Tribulation. What is it? Tribulation is pressure coming from outside, such as opposition, attack, ostracism, oppression, scourging, pillaging, and so forth.

(2) Poverty. People do not feel too bad if they are amply supplied financially during tribulation. But to suffer tribulation together with poverty can in fact be considered as reaching the end of the road.

In spite of such a situation, the Lord adds a most precious word, saying, "but thou art rich"—At that time her faith is really rich (James 2.5) and her love is truly full (1 Thess. 1.3). Otherwise, who would not indeed fall under such circumstances?

The church in Smyrna is directly contrary to the church in Laodicea (3.17). Now no one can be Smyrna before the Lord and simultaneously be Laodicea before the world.

(3) Words of blasphemy. This is that which defames us. Some people may endure tribulation and poverty, but few can withstand the mocking of their name.

"The blasphemy of them that say they are Jews"—This is because such blasphemy is begun by the Jews. Even while our Lord was on earth He was so blasphemed; how then can *we* avoid it?

What are the blasphemers' words? Blasphemy against

the word of salvation (Acts 13.45, 18.6, 19.9, 28.22; Rom. 3.8). Yet the Lord says "Blessed are ye when men shall . . . say all manner of evil against you falsely, for my sake" (Matt. 5.11).

Something more can be noticed here: "Say they are Jews, and they are not, but are a synagogue of Satan"— Who are these people? Before solving this puzzle, we should first find out who are the real Jews. By reading Romans 2.28–29, John 8.39–47, and Romans 4.11–12 we can readily perceive that a true believer in the Lord Jesus is a real Jew. Thus, those who are not Jews but say they are will naturally be a stance which points to the Jews according to the flesh together with the proselytes converted to Judaism.

These people are organized into what may be called the Judaized church. Their teachings are Judaized, being partly based on law and partly on grace, a salvation partly by faith and partly by works. Their system follows that which is under the law, with a priestly caste. There were a great number of these people at Paul's time; except that they were more developed and organized by the time of Revelation. Thus they have now become a synagogue of Satan, being used by him to propagate another gospel which is not the gospel at all.

2.10 "Fear not the things which thou art about to suffer"—These are the things which they will yet suffer, additional to the three things before mentioned. This is truly suffering upon suffering. But the Lord has told us beforehand.

"Fear not": (1) Fear is the source of defeat. Fearlessness precludes defeat. (2) Since the Lord has already overcome, we too—though we suffer—will eventually overcome.

"Behold, the devil is about to cast some of you into prison, that ye may be tried"—In the beginning it is but opposition and blasphemy; but later it is increased to include imprisonment. The purposes behind imprisonment are (1) that they may not be able to witness outside, so as to bind the truth of the Lord; (2) that they may be separated from one another, thus diminishing their strength; and (3) that those imprisoned may so suffer as to faint in their heart. Oh! How venomous are the wiles of the devil.

"The devil is about . . ."—No man is mentioned, only the devil is especially pointed out here. This is so that (1) we will not murmur against men but will hate the devil, and (2) we may recognize the enemy and resist him.

"And ye shall have tribulation ten days"—The "ten days" cited does not refer to a literal ten days and ten nights. It simply tells us that this suffering of ours has its time limit. It may also typify the ten colossal persecutions that were perpetrated by the Roman Empire.

"Be thou faithful unto death"—(1) "Unto death" indicates the possibility of being killed. When the devil discovers that imprisonment fails to achieve its aim he will move a step further, namely, to killing. (2) "Be thou" is cast in the imperative mood, being a command. (3) "Faithful unto death" means that they love not their lives even to death (Rev. 12.11). Such is the limit of the devil's attack. He cannot do anything further if we are thus faithful.

"And I will give thee the crown of life"—What a precious promise, what a blessed hope is this (James 1.12). What is promised here is not just life, but the *crown* of life. Life is received through believing; the crown of life is obtained by being faithful.

"Crown" speaks of glory, reigning with the Lord in the kingdom of the heavens.

2.11 "He that hath an ear, let him hear what the Spirit saith to the churches"—This has already been explained. "He that overcometh shall not be hurt of the second death"—How clear is the promise to the overcomer told: positively, obtaining the crown of life; negatively, not to be hurt of the second death.

"He that overcometh shall not be hurt of the second death"—Put conversely, it would read: The one who is overcome will be hurt by the second death. However, before "hurt of the second death" is mentioned, the word first specifies what the victory or defeat here is. The victory here is a being faithful unto death, so naturally the defeat will be an unwillingness to be a martyr for the Lord. One who loves his own life and does not dare to die for the Lord will be hurt by the second death.

Now let us ask what the second death is. In 20.14,15 we are told that the dead after being resurrected will be cast into the lake of fire, which is eternal perdition. Believers, though, will have no part in it (John 10.28).

The *hurt* of the second death and the second death itself are different. As life is in opposition to second death, so the crown of life is in contrast to the hurt of the second death. Since there is a difference between life and the crown of life, there must also be a distinction between the second death and the hurt of the second death. Furthermore, our knowing that the crown of life pertains to the kingdom will cause us to see that the hurt of the second death quite naturally falls within the kingdom period too. And hence the *hurt* of the second death cannot mean eternal perdition.

Let us now define directly what the hurt of the second death is and what the second death itself is. The second death denotes that a non-believer whose soul has already suffered after death will suffer eternally in spirit and soul and body after being resurrected in the future. The hurt of the second death simply means that a believer after being resurrected may suffer during the kingdom age, though this is assuredly not eternal perdition. Here I will praise God for His righteousness, for an overcomer having suffered martyrdom on earth shall not be hurt by the second death during the kingdom time but will receive instead the crown of life. Yes, a defeated Christian who is unwilling to die for the Lord may escape suffering on earth, but will be hurt at the kingdom period and shall not receive the crown of life. Who would not rather choose to suffer now and receive glory then?

An Old Testament typology may help to illustrate this point. The people in Sodom were burned to death—and this may signify the second death. Lot's wife was turned into a pillar of salt outside the city—but this may suggest the *hurt* of the second death.

2.12-17 THE CHURCH IN PERGAMUM

This church signifies the condition of the church from the fourth to the seventh century.

2.12 "And to the angel of the church in Pergamum write: These things saith he that hath the sharp two-edged sword"—Pergamum in the original Greek means (1) "united in marriage", which indicates the relationship between the church and the world; and (2) "high tower" (or "fortified"), which points to the position of the church in the world.

"He that hath the sharp two-edged sword"—The sharp sword has two functions: one is to cut asunder the union between the church and the world, and the other is to judge that church which is united to the world.

2.13 "I know where thou dwellest"—The church sojourns on earth as a passer-by just as our Lord too was

once a stranger in this world. How pitiful that the church
now has lost her character as a sojourner and has instead a
dwelling, that is, a position here. This shows how the
church has become worldly, and her dwelling is in Pergamum—which means high tower, that is to say, having a
superior position, influence and glory.

Judging by outward appearance, the church is most
prosperous, possessing position, influence and glory; but in
reality she has been corrupted and defeated. For although
the duty of the church on earth is to battle against the
enemy, she now owns a dwelling place where the seat of
Satan is. In other words, Satan occupies a place in the
church. How lamentable this is!

"In the days of Antipas my witness, my faithful one,
who was killed among you, where Satan dwelleth"—In
these seven letters, no believer's name is ever mentioned
except that of Antipas. Thus is affirmed the extreme
importance of this believer. Why was Antipas killed? For
the sake of holding fast the Lord's name and not denying
his faith. That is, he was killed because he faithfully
testified to these facts.

"And thou holdest fast my name, and didst not deny my
faith"—As long as Antipas lived, and through his faithful
standing, the whole church stood firm. But after he was
killed, the entire church was shaken.

2.14 "But I have a few things against thee, because
thou hast there some that hold the teaching of Balaam, who
taught Balak to cast a stumbling block before the children
of Israel, to eat things sacrificed to idols, and to commit
fornication"—Balaam was a covetous Old Testament
prophet whose teaching aimed at uniting the Israelites with
the Gentiles. How very many there are today who preach
for the sake of money, and how they advocate a union with

the world. As Balaam was hired by Balak, even so, since the time of Constantine the Great, many others have been employed by kings. The effects of the teaching of Balaam are: (1) eating things sacrificed to idols, which is to say, to be mixed with other religions, and (2) committing fornication, which in other words is to befriend the world.

2.15 "So hast thou also some that hold the teaching of the Nicolaitans in like manner"—Since the period typified was the time when the Roman Empire accepted Christianity as her religion, and since most of the people had no knowledge of Christian truths, naturally the burden of carrying on spiritual things fell on a minority. Class system became a necessity, and soon this system developed into a kind of teaching.

2.16 "Repent therefore, or else I come to thee quickly, and I will make war against them with the sword of my mouth"—The sword in verse 12 is the word of the Lord which will cut asunder our relationship with the world. If we hear His admonition but do not repent and sever our relationship with the world, we will be judged by His sword-like word.

2.17 "He that hath an ear, let him hear what the Spirit saith to the churches. To him that overcometh, to him will I give of the hidden manna, and I will give him a white stone, and upon the stone a new name written, which no one knoweth but he that receiveth it"—Here are two promises for the overcomer, namely: (1) The hidden manna. Manna is a type of Christ (John 6.49–51). The visible manna was shared in by all the children of Israel, but the hidden manna was to be preserved for Canaan. All believers enjoy the salvation of Christ, but only the overcomers partake of that hidden part of Christ which is not known by all. (2) A white stone. During those days a white stone—on which was written the name of a candidate —was used for election, and then it was deposited in an urn. Though an overcomer will obviously not be elected by the religious world, he will nonetheless receive from the Lord a white stone on which is inscribed a new name unknown to all the rest. This indicates the Lord's satisfaction with us.

2.18–29 THE CHURCH IN THYATIRA

This church represents the Roman Catholic system.

2.18 "And to the angel of the church in Thyatira write: These things saith the Son of God, who hath his eyes like a flame of fire, and his feet are like unto burnished brass"—The Lord identifies himself as (1) One whose eyes are like a flame of fire that can see through and distinguish all things, and (2) the Son of God, thus reminding the Roman Catholic Church of her error of inordinately uplifting Mary. And His feet are like burnished brass which are capable of executing judgment. What His eyes condemn, His feet trample down.

2.19 "I know thy works, and thy love and faith and ministry and patience, and that thy last works are more than the first"—We are most surprised to hear of the many good works to be found in such a corrupted church. Naturally, these are performed by a relative few. In spite of the failure of the great majority there are still a few who are excellent. This may be proved by looking at church history.

[*Translator's Note:* As was indicated in the Preface to this English translation of Mr. Nee's study on the book of

Revelation, that part of the study dealing with chapter 2.19 through 3.22 was found missing. For the sake of completion, therefore, the reader will find, in the paragraphs which follow, a re-arrangement of an English translation, made by the present translator, of the pertinent portion of one of the author's later works published in Chinese, entitled *Church Orthodoxy*. This translated portion is taken directly from the first Chinese edition of the work, which was published at Chungking in 1945.]

The Lord does acknowledge that there is some reality even in the Roman Catholic system. People such as Madame Guyon, François Fenelon, La Combe, John Tauler, and many others were not only saved but knew God in a real way as well. This is something for us to remember.

2.20 "But I have this against thee, that thou sufferest the woman Jezebel . . . ; and she teacheth and seduceth my servants to commit fornication, and to eat things sacrificed to idols"—Who is this Jezebel?

Jezebel, whose story is recorded in 1 Kings, was an unusual Old Testament personality. Ahab King of Israel took to wife this Jezebel, the daughter of a Sidonian king (1 Kings 16.31). She seduced the people into serving and worshiping another god, even Baal. The problem created at that time was more than simply a worshiping of idols; the children of Israel had also changed their God. They made Baal their god. Never before had there been any king to lead Israel to sin more than King Ahab. He was the first one who steered the people along to worship a foreign god. His sin surpassed even that of Jeroboam.

The woman here mentioned is Jezebel. Both the woman mentioned in Revelation 17 and the woman who hid the leaven in three measures of meal as mentioned in Matthew 13 betoken the Roman Catholic system.

Here is a woman who brings confusion to God's people as well as to God's word. She brings in idolatry. She calls herself a prophetess. She desires to preach and to teach. It is quite true that according to divine truth the church stands before God in the position of a woman. But whenever the church assumes the authority to teach, she turns into a Jezebel. The church of God has no right to speak on her own. In other words, the church has no doctrine of her own, since only the Son of God is the truth and has truths. Christ as the Head of the church alone can speak. How the Roman Catholic system, having turned into a Jezebel, insists on what the church says instead of what the Bible says or what the Lord says.

Jezebel has committed adultery—she has joined herself to the world. The phenomenon of the Roman Catholic system for the past thousand and some odd years is, according to the epistle of James (4.4), an adultery of the first magnitude. Here we find that the church has lost her chastity.

The consequence of such adultery is idol-worship. We are faced with the fact that none other than the Roman Catholic Church has so many idols.

"Thou sufferest the woman Jezebel . . . ; and she teacheth and seduceth my servants to commit fornication, and to eat things sacrificed to idols"—Why Jezebel? Because she introduces foreign gods and so can represent the Roman Catholic Church. How foreign deities have been taken over and labeled with Christian names, the most notable being the image of Mary. The Greeks had the goddess Venus, the eastern countries had the goddess of mercy, the Egyptians had the goddess of the nether region, but only Christianity had no goddess. For the sake of having a goddess, therefore, Mary was introduced. This is idolatry added on to fornication. The failure of the believers at Thyatira, says God, is to allow such teaching to prevail over them.

2.21 "And I gave her time that she should repent; and she willest not to repent of her fornication"—There is only one woman in the whole world who has killed the prophets, and she is Jezebel. During the middle centuries, countless numbers of God's children died a martyr's death at the hand of the Roman Catholic Church. She insists that what she decides or judges is right, and she tries to control man's thought. She will not repent.

2.22 "Behold, I cast her into a bed"—Notice that this is not a coffin, but a bed. It means she is fixed for life, just as a physician might declare the sickness of a patient to be terminal. Her condition will not improve.

2.23 "I will kill her children with death; and all the churches shall know that I am he that searcheth the reins and hearts: and I will give unto each one of you according to your works"—This may refer to how God in the future will use Antichrist and his party to destroy the Roman Catholic system.

2.24,25 "But to you I say, to the rest that are in Thyatira, as many as have not this teaching, who know not the deep things of Satan, as they are wont to say; I cast upon you none other burden. Nevertheless that which ye have, hold fast till I come"—Notice the phrase "the rest that are in Thyatira": Jezebel wanted to kill Elijah. The latter was greatly disappointed and afraid, so he hid himself. When questioned by God, he complained that he alone was left and yet his life was in danger. God's answer to him was:

He had seven thousand in Israel who had not bent their knees to Baal (1 Kings 19). These are "the rest that are in Thyatira".

Thank God, there are still those who "have not this teaching, who know not the deep things of Satan"—The word "bathea" in Greek is translated "mystery" or "deep things" in English. If you ask a Catholic priest whether you can take the Bible and comment on it, you will often be told that the Bible is such a mystery that none but the Pope is able to understand it. To those who do not follow such teaching the Lord puts no burden upon them save to keep what they have already learned of Him. It is enough just to keep it until He comes.

2.26,27 "And he that overcometh, and he that keepeth my works unto the end, to him will I give authority over the nations: and he shall rule them with a rod of iron, as the vessels of the potter are broken to shivers; as I also have received of my Father"—This is the first promise. In the kingdom to come, he who overcomes today shall rule the nations with an iron rod.

What God creates is stone, but what man produces is brick. From the time of the tower of Babel to the time as described in 2 Timothy, all who counterfeit God's work are considered vessels of clay. They shall be broken one by one until the arrival of the new heaven and the new earth.

2.28 "And I will give him the morning star"—This is the second promise. Physically speaking, we know the morning star in the sky is Venus. It has two characteristics: it being the first star to appear in the sky at dawn as well as being the first one at dusk. One day the Lord shall be seen by the whole world (Mal. 4.2—"the sun of righteousness [shall] arise"). But those who see the morning star are necessarily awake much earlier while the vast majority are still asleep. And these who see the morning star are the overcomers.

2.29 "He that hath an ear, let him hear what the Spirit saith to the churches"—The Lord speaks not only to the Roman Catholic Church but to all the churches as well. In the three preceding letters the call for overcomers always follows the words "he that hath an ear, let him hear"; but beginning with Thyatira, this order is reversed. This indicates that the first three churches belong to one class while the last four churches compose another class. The history of Smyrna commences after that of Ephesus has ended, and so too begins the history of Pergamum after that of Smyrna has finished. Thyatira comes after the history of Pergamum is closed, but Thyatira does not pass off the scene when Sardis arrives. Instead, Thyatira, Sardis, Philadelphia and Laodicea will all continue even to the second coming of the Lord Jesus.

3.1-6 THE CHURCH IN SARDIS

As the church falls progressively, from the works of the Nicolaitans at the Apostolic age to the domination of the prophetess Jezebel in the Roman Catholic system, God can no longer tolerate it. Hence comes Sardis. Sardis means "restoration" in the Greek. Sardis is God's reaction to Thyatira. The history of revivals is the story of divine reactions. Whenever God starts to do the work of revival, He is reacting against the status quo. Now God's reaction is man's recovery.

3.1 "The things saith he that hath the seven Spirits of God, and the seven stars"—In Ephesus the Lord holds the

seven stars in His right hand, in Sardis He has the seven
stars. Ephesus is the deterioration of the Apostolic age,
while Sardis is the recovery from Thyatira. Works without
love is Ephesus, and name without life is Sardis. So these
two form a pair.

The seven Spirits are sent by God to the world to do the
works of life. In Ephesus the seven stars point to the
messengers, but here they signify enlightening. Revival
work is done partly in the Spirit and partly in the light.
Sardis, we can therefore say, represents the history of the
Protestant church from the Reformation until the Lord's
return.

"I know thy works, that thou hast a name that thou
livest, and thou art dead"—No one will ever be doubtful of
Luther as God's servant; nor will any be skeptical of the
Reformation as a magnificent piece of God's work, as a
divine reaction. When Luther began his work, it was Sardis.
His motive was wholly for restoration.

3.2 "Be thou watchful, and establish the things that
remain, which were ready to die: for I have found no works
of thine perfected before my God"—The Lord does not say
that Luther's work is not good, He only says it is not
perfected, all having good beginnings yet without ends.
Being the perfect Lord that He is, He demands perfection.

With the Reformation we have justification by faith
restored as well as an open Bible; but in the matter of the
church, the Reformation still imitates Rome instead of
returning to the status of the early church. This is history.
The Reformation leaves the church matter unsolved.
Luther himself did not consider justification by faith
sufficient to make the Reformation complete, for there were
things concerning the church that were left for others to
tackle. Yet we have stopped short. Though we have

returned to the faith once delivered to the saints, still there is no formidable change in the status of the church. The churches in the Reformation became united to various nations. As Thyatira is married to the world, so Sardis is united to different nations.

In the eighteenth century there began the history of the dissenters. Those who did not wish to follow national lines used instead doctrines as their lines of demarkation.

"Thou hast a name that thou livest, and thou art dead. Be thou watchful, and establish the things that remain, which were ready to die"—This refers to justification by faith and the open Bible. In the entire history of Sardis these are seen to be dying, and the Lord therefore exhorts the believers to establish the things which remain.

3.3 "Remember therefore how thou hast received and didst hear; and keep it, and repent"—The history of Protestantism is one of revivals. Today Protestantism acts as though it were a cup. Whenever there is God's blessing, people will organize themselves so as to contain it. Though the blessing of God is still there, it is being circumscribed. During the first generation, the cup is full; with the second generation, however, it is only half full, so that the message becomes less clear; and by the third or fifth generation, there is no more water but only the cup remains. People then contend about whose cup is best, yet no one can obtain anything to drink. And the result: God answers with another reaction, and so another Sardis is born.

Man always tries to set up something to preserve God's grace. Now the cup of man's making will never be broken because it never lacks people who will exert themselves to maintain it. So that the entire history is one of revivals. On the one hand there is revival, for which we are thankful to God. On the other hand, in these revivals man never returns to the beginning; and consequently we believers are reprimanded by God. God's servants have this one problem, that they find it extremely difficult to distinguish between what is living water and what is an empty cup. And so from each old cup there continually evolves some new cup. Protestantism, then, is always experiencing revival, yet the Lord declares it to be imperfect. It is almost perfect, but not quite, since it never has gone back to the beginning.

"Remember therefore how thou hast received and didst hear"—The question is not how *now* to receive and hear, rather how things were received and heard *then*. "And they continued stedfastly in the apostles' teaching and fellowship" (Acts 2.42). We cannot invent a fellowship. The apostles' fellowship is the fellowship of Christ. If it is the apostles' teaching, it is in fact Christ's teaching. The error with Thyatira was to create her own teaching. Yet God has not charged us to invent, only to receive. During the past 20 centuries everything could be invented except truth. We may *discover* truth in our spirit, but we can never *invent* any truth.

"I will come as a thief, and thou shalt not know what hour I will come upon thee"—The coming of a thief is a coming *upon* (Greek, *epi*) which means coming *by* you, but you do not know it. Many brethren in the past have rightly observed that the thief comes to steal the best. Even so too will the Lord steal the very best from the earth. Only the best will be in his hand: "One is taken, and one is left" (Matt. 24.40–41). Hence He says, "If therefore thou shalt not watch, I will come as a thief" (3.3).

3.4 "But thou hast a few names in Sardis that did not defile their garments: and they shall walk with me in white; for they are worthy"—The Lord pays special attention to our names. When we stand before God we are clothed with Christ, for He is our white garment. But when we stand before Christ at His judgment seat we need to be clothed also in "fine linen, bright and pure: for the fine linen is the righteousnesses of the saints" (Rev. 19.8 Darby). The word "righteousnesses" is plural in number.

3.5 "He that overcometh shall thus be arrayed in white garments; and I will in no wise blot his name out of the book of life, and I will confess his name before my Father, and before his angels"—Here it is not a matter of having a name written but a matter of having a name confessed. At the time of resurrection the angels will also be present. And he whom the Lord confesses has part in the kingdom, but he whose name is not recognized by the Lord has no portion in the kingdom. Now this is not a question of eternity, it is a question of reigning with Christ. How pathetic it will be to have one's name written in the book of life and yet not confessed!

3.7-13 THE CHURCH IN PHILADELPHIA

The name "Philadelphia" is a combination of two Greek words "philo" and "adelphos": "philo" means "love", and "adelphos" means "brother": and hence Philadelphia signifies "brotherly love". Now you will notice that the words of the Lord to Philadelphia and to Smyrna are quite alike. Of the seven churches, five are reprimanded, and only two receive no reproof. These two are Smyrna and Philadelphia. Just as the trouble in Smyrna came from Judaism and the Jews, so the same is true with Philadelphia. To the church in Smyrna the Lord says: "Ye shall have tribulation"; to the church in Philadelphia He says: "I also will keep thee from the hour of trial, the hour which is to come upon the whole world." To both of these churches the Lord mentions the crown. To Smyrna He says: "I will give thee the crown of life"; and to Philadelphia He says: "Hold fast that which thou hast, that no one take thy crown."

Since these two churches have many similarities, they stand in the same line: the orthodox line of the Apostles. But though the church in Sardis is truly a restoration, the recovery is not perfect. For unlike the church in Philadelphia which receives praises, Sardis receives reproaches. We thus know for sure that Philadelphia is the Lord's choice because it is an extension of the orthodox line of the Apostles.

In the last century just past we have had a great movement in the church which surpasses the Reformation. And thus Philadelphia has given us that which the Reformation failed to give. We thank God, for the matter of the church is solved through the early Brethren movement. The position of God's children is almost entirely restored. Nevertheless, the fame of the Brethren movement falls far behind that of the Reformation. For the Reformation broke upon the world with the aid of sword and gun, whereas the Brethren movement depended purely on the preaching of the word of God.

3.7 "And to the angel of the church in Philadelphia write"—Philadelphia: brotherly love. In what respect does God particularly praise Philadelphia? In their brotherly love, for the intermediary class that distinguished clergy from laity has been totally abolished. Moreover, in the church there are neither Jews nor Gentiles, neither freemen nor bondmen. All are brothers. Only after our eyes have been opened to this can brotherly love ever be possible. In the world, distinctions are glorious; but in the church, it is shameful. The church stands not on distinctions but on brotherly love.

"These things saith he that is holy, he that is true, he that hath the key of David, he that openeth and none shall shut, and that shutteth and none openeth"—Holy is the Lord's life; He himself is that holiness. And He is that reality before God, for He is God's reality. The key of David means authority. Christ is the finality, and all problems are solved in Him. It is not a matter of force, nor of advertising, but of His opening the door.

3.8 "I know thy works . . . , that thou hast a little power"—One passage in the Scriptures may be associated with this verse: "Who hath despised the day of small things?" (Zech. 4.10) You should not despise the day of small things, that is, the day of the rebuilding of the temple. After the seventy years of captivity the remnant of the Jews returned to Jerusalem in weakness and in groups. They rebuilt the holy temple, thus serving as a type of the Brethren movement. Many of the older Jews who had seen the old temple wept with a loud voice when they saw the foundation of the house of God being laid. For how could the glory of this temple be compared with the glory of the temple of Solomon? But God spoke through the prophet Zechariah, saying that they ought not despise the day of small things. Comparatively speaking, the testimony of the church in the world is like a day of small things.

"And didst keep my word, and didst not deny my name"—On the side of strength, the Lord grants them two things: the keeping of His word and no denying of His name. The Brethren are noted for their knowledge of God's word. A simple believer among them appears to have a clearer understanding of the Scriptures than some missionaries. And since 1828 the Brethren have maintained that they can only be called Christians. Many people insist on having denominational names, but these brethren have no other name than Christian. That they are called by the name Brethren (with a capital "B") by others is something which they have never called themselves.

"Behold, I have set before thee a door opened, which none can shut"—To Philadelphia the Lord only mentions "open". People may contend that if you preach according to the Scriptures all doors will be shut. The greatest hardship in obeying the Lord is when a person finds doors closed. Yet here is this extraordinary promise: "Behold, I have set before Thee a door opened, which none can shut"!

3.9 "Behold, I give of the synagogue of Satan, of them that say they are Jews, and they are not, but do lie; behold, I will make them to come and worship before thy feet, and to know that I have loved thee"—There are at least four things which Judaizes Christianity; namely, an intermediary priesthood, a written code, a physical temple, and earthly promises. For those who truly know God, the influence of Judaism is completely nullified.

3.10 "Because thou didst keep the word of my patience"—This is joined with "partaker with you in the tribulation and kingdom and patience which are in Jesus" (1.9). The word here is a noun, not an adjective: It is not My patient word, but the word of My patience, which is to say, the patience of Christ himself. Today the Lord is patient with those who revile Him. His word is the word of patience. He has no fame here on this earth. He is a humble Man, the Man of Nazareth, supposed to be the son of a carpenter. As we follow Him, we are told to keep the word of His patience.

"I also will keep thee from the hour of trial, that hour which is to come upon the whole world, to try them that dwell upon the earth"—The trial which is to come upon the whole world, all Christians know, is the Great Tribulation. But before the hour of trial is come we shall already be raptured. In the Bible there are two places which speak of the *promise* of rapture: one is found in Luke 21.36 and the other is in Revelation 3.10. We need to follow the Lord carefully, learn to walk in the way of Philadelphia, and ask the Lord to deliver us from all these things that are coming upon the world.

3.11 "I come quickly: hold fast that which thou hast, that no one take thy crown"—This church shall continue on until the Lord's return. "Hold fast that which thou hast"—What do the Philadelphians have? My word, My name. "That no one take thy crown"—To the other churches, it is a question of *gaining* the crown; to Philadelphia, it is a question of *losing* it. For the Lord says, you already have the crown. There is only one person in the whole New Testament who knew he had the crown, and that man was Paul. And of all the churches, Philadelphia alone knows she has the crown. Now then, says the Lord, do not let anybody take it away; by which He meant, do not come out of Philadelphia and forsake her place.

3.12 "He that overcometh, I will make him a pillar in the temple of my God, and he shall go out thence no more: and I will write upon him the name of my God, and the name of the city of my God, the new Jerusalem, which cometh down out of heaven from my God, and mine own new name"—Just as Philadelphia frequently experienced ostracism in her history, so she will one day not be excommunicated any more. To be a pillar in the temple of

God means to be permanently settled, because a pillar cannot be taken away. Philadelphia, like a pillar, will support the temple of God, having the three names of God, New Jerusalem, and Christ inscribed on her. The eternal purpose of God is then fulfilled. The Philadelphians satisfy the Lord as well as belong to the Lord.

3.13 "He that hath an ear, let him hear what the Spirit saith to the churches"—Remember well that God has not given us alternatives to choose from; rather, He has laid out most plainly before us the way of the church.

3.14-22   THE CHURCH IN LAODICEA

To what does the church in Laodicea point? Many are unable to answer this question. Some may try to glean personal lessons from it, others may take it as representing the ruinous situation of the church in general. But the Lord is here prophesying.

3.14 "And to the angel of the church in Laodicea write"—Her name is quite peculiar. It is a combination of two Greek words: *Laos,* meaning "people" or "laity"; and *dicea* meaning "opinion" or "custom": hence Laodicea means the opinion or the custom of the people. We can see very distinctly that the church has fallen. What we see in Philadelphia is love, what we see in Philadelphia is the brethren. But here everything has become common. If God's people do not stand stedfastly in the position of Philadelphia, they will change. Yet they will never change by returning to Sardis; instead, they will become Laodicea. That which comes out of Rome (Thyatira) is Protestantism (Sardis), that which comes out of Protestantism is the brethren (Philadelphia). And that which comes out of the brethren becomes the laity (Laodicea).

One day when the brethren fail to stand firm on the ground of the brethren, they fall from *adelphos* (brethren) to *laos* (laity or people). In Sardis, authority is in the hand of the pastors. In Philadelphia, authority falls on the brethren. Now, though, in Laodicea it is neither with the brethren nor with the pastors but with the laity. This means the opinion of the majority. In the people, you meet Laodicea; in the Lord's will, you see Philadelphia.

"These things saith the Amen, the faithful and true witness, the beginning of the creation of God"—Philadelphia and Laodicea are similar in church position. The difference lies in the fact that Philadelphia has love. There is not much distinction in outward appearance; what differentiates them is that Laodicea is a proud Philadelphia. Only fallen Philadelphia can become Laodicea. Riches themselves are the characteristic of Philadelphia; *boasting* of being rich is the trademark of Laodicea. The fatal disease with Laodicea is pride.

The Lord speaks of himself here as the Amen, the faithful and true witness, and the beginning of God's creation. Everything that the Lord has mentioned will find its fulfillment in Him. As a matter of fact, all that is of God shall be accomplished in Him. The Lord came to the world to bear witness to the work of God. He is the Head over all things.

3.15,16 "I know thy works, that thou art neither cold nor hot: I would thou wert cold or hot. So because thou art lukewarm, and neither hot nor cold, I will spew thee out of my mouth"—Sardis has a name of being alive and yet is dead; Laodicea is neither cold nor hot. In Ephesus it is "move thy candlestick out of its place"; here it is "spew thee out of my mouth": the Lord will have no more use of her.

3.17 "Because thou sayest, I am rich, and have gotten riches, and have need of nothing; and knowest not that thou art the wretched one and miserable and poor and blind and naked"—They have reason to be proud on the natural plane; but spiritual things ought to inhibit boasting. As soon as there is boasting, things spiritual vanish. The word "wretched" is the same as found in Romans 7.24: "Wretched man that I am!" The Lord is saying: you are spiritually wretched as is the man in Romans 7. In the eyes of the Lord they are pitiful. Three reasons are thereafter given for their wretchedness and misery: they are in reality poor and naked and blind.

3.18 "I counsel thee to buy of me gold refined by fire, that thou mayest become rich; and white garments, that thou mayest clothe thyself, and that the shame of thy nakedness be not made manifest; and eyesalve to anoint thine eyes, that thou mayest see"—In order to deal with the above three curses they must buy gold, white garments, and eyesalve.

In God's view, richness in doctrine is useless; consequently, they are still poor. The Lord exhorts them to buy gold refined by fire that they may be rich. In his first epistle Peter says: "The proof of your faith, being more precious than gold that perisheth though it is proved by fire" (1.7).

"White garments" refers to works or conduct. God's will is for them to be undefiled like wearing white garments, so that they may always walk before Him. The problem here is not whether there is a garment to wear, but whether the garment is white. "And whosoever shall give to drink unto one of these little ones a cup of cold water only, in the name of a disciple", says the Lord Jesus, "verily I say unto you he shall in no wise lose his reward" (Matt. 10.42). This is the white garment. The Lord wishes people to do His works with a pure enough motive. How many activities are done with impure motives!

Eyesalve speaks of the revelation of the Holy Spirit. One only sees when he has the Holy Spirit's revelation. Too much understanding on doctrine may impede the Holy Spirit's revelation. How many are walking in the light of other people! May we learn this before God: to buy eyesalve.

3.19 "As many as I love, I reprove and chasten: be zealous therefore, and repent"—All that has been said before are words of reproach, but the Lord now shows us that He reproves and chastens because He loves. Not only individuals need to repent, the church also must repent.

3.20 "Behold, I stand at the door and knock: if any man hear my voice and open the door, I will come in to him, and will sup with him, and he with me"—What is this door? There are two possibilities: one is the heart door, the other is the door of the church. Many use this Scripture verse to preach the gospel. We certainly can borrow this verse to preach the gospel to sinners, but we must not borrow it forever without returning it to its proper context. Strictly speaking, the Lord is speaking of the door of the church. How strange it is that the Lord who is the head of the church is now standing *outside* the door of the church. "Behold, I stand at the door and knock"—The word "behold" is addressed to the whole church, but the message is spoken to individuals. The door is the door of the church, but hearing His voice and opening the door come from the individuals.

We know that truth has two sides: the subjective and the objective, experience versus truth. The biggest failure of the Brethren is to overemphasize objective truth. "I will come in to him, and will sup with him, and he with me"—This implies that the Lord will turn all their objective truths into subjective experiences.

3.21 "He that overcometh, I will give to him to sit down with me in my throne, as I also overcame, and sat down with my Father in his throne"—Many people consider this to be the best among all the promises given to the overcomers of the seven churches. Why is the overcomer promised such a noble thing? Because the church age shall soon be over, and the overcomer is waiting for the return of the Lord. For this reason, we see the throne.

[Here ends the translated portion taken directly from Mr. Nee's *Church Orthodoxy* (First Chinese edition, Chungking, 1945) covering Revelation 2.19 to 3.22 of this present study.—*Translator*]

PART THREE

THE SCENES AT THE THRONE

The Scenes at the Throne
(4.1–5.14)

On the basis of the words "After these things", some maintain that whatever is described in chapters 4 and 5 are events yet to be fulfilled, since these two chapters speak of the things which will happen at the time when the church shall be raptured and the Lord shall return immediately. Such an interpretation is most widely accepted, but it presents the following eight problems.

(1) If chapters 4 and 5 truly refer to "the things which shall come to pass hereafter", why should such a significant event as the rapture of the church not be mentioned? Rapture is touched upon in chapters 7, 12, 14 and 15 of this book. Why is it not referred to here? Some do suggest that the rapture of the church is implied in the words "Come up hither" (4.1), but are not these words followed immediately by "Straightway I was in the Spirit . . ." (v.2)? The rapture of the church is a bodily rapture, yet here it is in the Spirit. And thus this verse cannot be interpreted as referring to the rapture of the church. How can chapters 2 and 3 speak of the church and there not be a clear word given of her rapture immediately afterwards?

(2) If 4.1 indeed speaks of the rapture of the church, then where is the church seen in chapters 4 and 5? Some people advance the thought that the 24 elders in 4.4,10 and 5.8 represent the church. We shall prove later on that they

do not represent the church. For the present we need only to ask one question: Why is it that not even one of the 24 elders is mentioned from 19.5 through chapter 22? Is it possible that the church is limited to the time of tribulation and to the enjoyment in the kingdom, but that she will not be heard of in the new heaven and the new earth? How can it be that she is seen at the beginning but she disappears at the end?

(3) Chapter 5 describes the glory which the Lamb receives in heaven. Can we say that the Lord must wait for about two thousand years before He will receive glory?

(4) The praise from every created thing which is in heaven and on the earth and under the earth spoken of in 5.13 agrees perfectly with what Philippians 2.10 says. Due to His resurrection and ascension and His receiving the Name that is above all names, He is shown in such glory as is described in Philippians (2.9). How, then, can it be said that Revelation 5.13 describes a scene of two thousand years later?

(5) Why should the new song in 5.9 be sung two thousand years later? Has not the work of redemption already been done? Why cannot the new song be sung at once?

(6) "As though it had been slain" (5.6) is, in the original, rendered "as though it had been *newly* slain"—This clearly proves that this is the scene of the ascension of the Lord. Although the death of the Lord is forever fresh, the word here designates it as being newly slain.

(7) In 4.8 the four living creatures are recorded as saying: "The Lord God, the Almighty, who was and who is and who is to come"—Compare this with 11.17, where the 24 elders are found worshiping God and saying: "O Lord God, the Almighty, who art and who wast"; in this latter instance the words "who is to come" are not said, thus

intimating that the return of the Lord cannot be before 4.8 but after 4.8.

(8) In 5.6 it is said that the seven Spirits of God are "sent forth into all the earth"—May we not ask, then, what the Holy Spirit will be doing in the great tribulation as He is sent out into all the earth? We know that the Holy Spirit comes down after the ascension of the Lord Jesus. It is during the dispensation of the church that He is sent out by the Lord.

In view of these eight points, we may conclude that chapter 4 depicts the daily scene in God's presence, which is the natural situation in heaven; while chapter 5 speaks of the sight of the Lord's ascension, for in it we are told of "a Lamb standing, as though it had been [newly] slain" (5.6). This scene is repeated for the benefit of the apostle John—"After these things . . . a door opened in heaven" (4.1). This is not a continuation of the seven churches but rather is a sequel to the vision given in chapter 1.

"A door opened in heaven"—The heavens were opened to Ezekiel (1.1), to the Lord (Matt. 3.16), to Stephen (Acts 7.56), to Peter (Acts 10.11) and to John (Rev. 4.1, 19.11).

"And the first voice that I heard, a voice as of a trumpet speaking with me"—It is not a trumpet blowing, but a voice *as* of a trumpet.

"Come up hither"—This word is spoken to John personally; it should not be interpreted as a type of the rapture of the church.

"I will show thee the things which must come to pass _ereafter"—This serves as an introduction to the prophecies to follow.

4.2,3 THE THRONE

4.2 "Straightway I was in the Spirit"—John was raptured in the spirit, it was not a bodily rapture.

"And behold, there was a throne set in heaven"—The throne is the heart of this book, it is also the focus of all things. The first thing to be seen, therefore, is the throne, since all the things which follow proceed from it. This is a different throne from that spoken of in the New Testament epistles. Hebrews 4, for example, speaks of the throne of grace—emphasizing the side of God's grace. But this is the throne of judgment here—emphasizing the side of God's righteousness.

"And one sitting upon the throne"—This one is none other than God.

4.3 "And he that sat was to look upon like a jasper stone and a sardius"—The better translation for "jasper" is "diamond".* Among precious stones, the one stone which resembles most the color of light is the diamond. It is unbreakable and most valued by mankind. It is formed out of carbon. Its light may be compared to the light of the gospel by which man is lifted out of darkness into marvelous light. "Sardius" has the most perfect red color. It therefore expresses the redemption of God, for blood is red in color. So, both of these precious stones, because of their colors, are used to represent both the light of the gospel and the redemption of God which is accomplished through the Lord Jesus.

"And there was a rainbow round about the throne, like an emerald to look upon"—The rainbow usually viewed on earth is bow-shaped, but the rainbow here surrounds the throne. Now the rainbow is the sign of God's covenant with

---

* "This is not considered to be the same as the modern jasper, which is an opaque variety of quartz of many different colors. To what gem Scripture refers is not known. Some suppose the diamond."—*A New and Concise Bible Dictionary* (London: G. Morrish, n.d., p. 405).—*Translator*

Noah, for God is a *keeper* of covenant as well as the God of covenant (Gen. 9.12–16). Here in Revelation we find that God is going to execute judgment soon; nevertheless, He still keeps His covenant and remembers His promises and grace. The green of an emerald is like the green grass. It is a major color on earth. Hence it shows that in judgment God has grace and He remembers the earth. After the earth has passed through judgment, it gives forth green color (Gen. 8.11).

4.4 "THE TWENTY-FOUR ELDERS"

The common interpretation of the 24 elders as given by most commentators is that they point to the entire glorious church. But do these commentators have sufficient proof for offering this interpretation? Recently some of them have quoted 4.4, saying that these elders have thrones and therefore they reign as kings; they also point out that in 5.8 these elders are shown as having harps and golden bowls full of incense, and hence they are priests. And does not 1 Peter 2.9 state that believers are "a royal priesthood"? Since these 24 elders are both kings and priests, surely, they conclude, these elders represent the glorious church.

According to this interpretation, therefore, the entire church must be raptured together and thus it does not go through the tribulation. But how, then, will 3.10 be explained? Furthermore, there are ten other reasons why the 24 elders do not represent one glorious church.

(1) The name of elder is not the name of the church. If the elders here point to the church, it will be almost like saying that the entire church is made up of elders. According to historical fact, God first chooses the angels (Is. 14.12; Ez. 28.11–19), then the Jews (Gen. 12.1–3), and thirdly the church (for it is formed in the time of Acts 2).

58 "Come, Lord Jesus"

Not only the church cannot be reckoned as elders, even the
Jews are not to be considered as elders (the election
mentioned in Ephesians 1.4 refers to the eternal purpose of
God, and hence is quite different from the elect angels as
mentioned in 1 Timothy 5.21).

(2) The number of the elders is not the number of the
church. The church's number in the Scriptures is seven or
multiples of seven, but 24 is not such a multiple.

(3) The church cannot have the throne and the crown
before the Lord Jesus has His. The one who sits on the
throne as seen in 4.2 is God the Father (the Lamb is
standing, according to 5.6). The 24 elders also sit on
thrones, and they all wear crowns of gold as described in
4.4. If they represent the church, how can it be that the
church sits while the Lamb stands? According to this
interpretation, in 5.6 the church is already crowned. Yet
please note that the Lord Jesus will not be King until the
time of chapter 20 is reached! How can the church receive
glory in advance of the Lord? Moreover, after 19.4 there is
no more trace of the 24 elders. If these elders do indeed
represent the entire church, what has happened to the
glorious church thereafter?

(4) The white garments which the elders wear are not
said to be cleansed by the precious blood; however, in
another place (7.14) the white garments are said to have
been washed and made white in the blood of the Lamb.
The white garments here show that the elders are without
sin.

(5) The song these elders sing is not that of redemption
since the song in 4.11 tells of the creation of God. They thus
know only God's creation; they have no personal knowledge of God's redemption. Though they do sing a new song
as mentioned in 5.9–10, this is because the Lord has

redeemed "them"—not these elders, but men of every tribe and tongue and people and nation.

(6) All the phenomena in chapter 4 stand for the state of the universe. Besides the throne and the seven Spirits, there are the four living creatures and the 24 elders; none else is mentioned. This indicates that these elders are the elders of the universe. Can we possibly say that the church is the eldest in the universe?

(7) To carry prayers to God as is shown in 5.8 is not the action of the church. Even though the church is commanded in the Scriptures to pray for others, God has not asked her to bring others' prayers to Him. The church does not have this power. Many commentators agree that the angel spoken of in 8.3–4 refers to the Lord. Whether or not it is the Lord, it can at least be said that the task of carrying prayers to God is done by angels. Thus, bringing prayers of the saints to God as mentioned in 5.8 must be a task done by the angels.

(8) Never once do the 24 elders identify themselves as the church. The "them" in 5.10 is a reference to the church by these elders. If the "them" were indeed an expression of self-identification, the elders should have instead said "us". What the elders do say clearly distinguishes them from the church. The 24 elders cannot represent the entire church. There are three classes of people in view in 7.13–17, namely: (1) elders, (2) John, and (3) those arrayed in white robes. Should the 24 elders be an allusion to *part* of the church, it would still make some sense for the elders to ask John, "Who are they, and whence came they [those in white robes]?" But if the 24 elders mean the entire church, it would be absurd for the entire church to ask concerning part of the church.

(9) John addresses one of the elders as "my lord" (7.13–

17), thus showing the superior position of the elder over John. Otherwise how could the elder permit John to call him "my lord"? (cf. 22.8–9)

(10) The demeanor of the 24 elders before God is most peculiar. They have never been hungry and thirsty like the church nor have they ever shed any tears. They are not afraid of God, neither do they possess any sense of sin. They are strangers to the experience of being redeemed. All these points prove that they are not the redeemed church.

Who, then, are these elders? Let us assume that they are the kings and priests among the angels, that they are the elders of the universe (that is to say, they rule over the angels and the universe in God's service). The evidences for such a conclusion are as follows.

(1) Since they sit on thrones and wear crowns of gold, they must be kings.

(2) They wear white garments which are the garments of the priests (see Ex. 28; Lev. 6.10, 16.4). They have harps, sing songs, and hold golden bowls of incense—all these are evidences of their priesthood.

(3) The reason they are the priests among the angels is because they are the elders of the universe. In chapters 4 and 5 God is God, the Lord is the Lamb, the Holy Spirit is the seven Spirits, the four living creatures represent the animate creation, and the 24 elders are the elders of the universe since they are the oldest among created things.

(4) Besides the angels, who are entitled to sit on thrones and wear golden crowns ahead of the Lord Jesus? God had originally appointed angels to govern the universe. But one of the archangels fell and turned himself into Satan, there thus coming into existence the satanic kingdom. As to those angels who had not followed Satan in rebellion, God still assigns them the rule over the universe. Now just as

Michael is the chief prince over the nation of Israel (Dan. 10.13), even so, all of us who are redeemed have our guardian angels (Acts 12.15; Matt. 18.10; Heb. 1.14). The 24 elders sit while the seven angels who blow the trumpets stand before God (8.2). They are now in charge of the universe. When they see people getting saved they are not jealous at all; rather, they praise God for it. They will govern the universe until the kingdom shall come; and then they will resign their appointments and there will be the transfer of the government of the universe to men (Rev. 11.16–18; Heb. 2.5–8). This is why there is no mentioning of the 24 elders after 19.4.

(5) The number of the 24 elders is the number of the priesthood. At the time of David the priesthood was divided into 24 courses (1 Chron. 24.7–18). The duty of the priesthood is to bring the prayers of the saints to God. The harps are for singing, and the golden bowls are for prayers.

4.5–6 THE SITUATION OF THE THRONE

4.5 "And out of the throne proceed lightnings and voices and thunders"—God is going to judge the world. Hence the throne here is God's throne of righteousness, the judicial throne of God.

"Lamps of fire" in the original is "torches of fire"—A lamp is for use in the house, whereas a torch is used for the outdoors. (The torch used by the Greeks was trumpet-shaped and filled with jute or cotton saturated with oil. It is used outdoors.)

The Holy Spirit is one Person in the Godhead; yet He is described here as the seven Spirits on the basis of His work and effect. This agrees perfectly with the meaning of the torches (see Rev. 5.6; Is. 11.2).

4.6 Why is "a sea of glass like unto crystal" before the throne? Because the rainbow which surrounds the throne is a memorial to God's promise at the time of Noah that the earth will no more be destroyed by water (Gen. 9.15). The judgment by water passed away; judgment is no longer executed by means of the sea. According to Revelation 15 the glassy sea seems to be "mingled with fire" (v.2). In the new heaven and the new earth there is no more sea. In eternity there will be only the lake of fire—a lake, yes, but one of fire. Robert Govett has observed that "the sea becomes the lake of fire. We are permitted to see it in its intermediate state in chapter 15, when it is a sea of glass mingled with fire." * What he has suggested appears reasonable.

Since there is but one throne, what is meant by "the midst of the throne" can only be a reference to the lower center before the throne.

"Full of eyes before and behind"—"Eyes" signify intelligence. By closing his eyes, a person will not be able to see the world. But that which has the most contact with the world is a person's eyes. To be full of eyes before and behind shows how very intelligent these living creatures are before God.

4.7,8 THE FOUR LIVING CREATURES

Some observers maintain that since the 24 elders represent the church, the four living creatures also stand for the church. But we do not think the book of Revelation is primarily a book of symbols. Whatever is not symbolic should be explained literally. If the 24 elders speak of the

---

* Robert Govett, *The Apocalypse Expounded.* London: Chas. J. Thynne, 1920, p. 111.—*Translator*

church, then how should the other numbers in the book be interpreted? Such an interpretation not only will be most difficult but also will impair the value of this book. Consequently, the four living creatures are not symbolic but are rather the representatives of the created things. As the 24 elders are representative of the angelic beings, so the four living creatures are representative of the living things on earth.

The classifications of the living creatures according to Genesis are six in number: (1) aquatics, (2) birds, (3) fowls, (4) creeping things, (5) beasts, and (6) man. But according to Revelation 4.7 there are only four kinds: (1) lion—the mightiest among beasts (Prov. 30.30); (2) calf—the biggest among domesticated animals; (3) man—the mankind on earth (this does not signify the church, for in the kingdom era the knowledge of God will fill the earth—see Is. 11.9). During that era there will be a difference in the church between the saved and the overcomers; but in the new heaven and the new earth there will no longer be such a difference. Though at the kingdom age men on earth may believe in God, there will be no baptism in the Holy Spirit, and hence they cannot become the body of Christ. They can only believe as individuals. In the new heaven and the new earth they will be restored to the state of Adam before the fall. They shall eat fruits, require sleep, enter into marriage, and beget children, though they will no longer die, be sick, sin, or be tempted by the devil. And (4) eagle—the king of birds.

Why are the creeping things and the fishes not mentioned here? Since the largest of the creeping things is the serpent, there is no representation. During the time of Noah the fishes had not passed through judgment (whereas all the other living creatures had); in addition, in the new heaven and the new earth there will be no more sea. Evidently fishes will be judged later; therefore, there is no representation.

Having been affected by the fall of man, creation has been corrupted quite far from its original state. And so, according to Romans 8.19–22, the whole creation earnestly awaits the revealing of the liberty of the glory of the children of God. When the Lord returns we shall be glorified, and the creation will be liberated from the bondage of corruption. At the coming of the Lord there will be the restoration of all things (Acts 3.21). The effect of our Lord's death on the cross is far reaching: it reaches to all things as well as to mankind (Col. 1.20). By reading Hebrews 2.5–9, we learn that Jesus "should taste of death for every man"; but "every man" ought to be rendered "every one" or "every thing" in verse 9. This means that Christ has tasted death for all things, even for the whole creation. Not only mankind, but the whole creation as well, will be redeemed.

The Lord Jesus is not only a man but also the firstborn of all creation (Col. 1.15; Rev. 3.14).

The four living creatures represent all the redeemed living things before God.

Now of the four living creatures both the calf and man are clean, whereas the lion and the eagle are unclean. Yet all of them stand before God without any differentiation between clean and unclean. The lion and the eagle are fierce while man and calf are mild-mannered. But because all are redeemed, all of them can dwell together in peace.

In the Old Testament there are two kinds of angelic beings mentioned: cherubim and seraphim. The cherubim have only four wings (Ez. 1.6), whereas the seraphim have six (Is. 6.2). The faces of the four living creatures are like the living creatures spoken of in Ezekiel. These four living creatures have the faces of the cherubim (Ez. 1.10) and the wings of the seraphim. Thus they are a composite of the cherubim and seraphim.

Cherubim stand for the glory of God (cherubim of gold mentioned in Exodus 37.7 signifies cherubim of glory), and seraphim stand for the holiness of God ("Holy, holy, holy" in Is. 6.3). Glory pertains to God himself, but holiness refers to God's nature. Hence, the four living creatures here are to manifest the glory and the holiness of God.

"And who is to come" means "the coming one"—This points to the second coming of the Lord.

4.9–11 PRAISES

4.9 There are "thanks" because the four living creatures also represent here all redeemed living things.

4.11 The 24 elders do not say "thanks" but say "power" instead, since they have no personal experience of salvation and they know only power. However, when they see the four living creatures praising God and giving thanks, they join in the worship without any sense of jealousy.

"For thou didst create all things, and because of thy will they were, and were created"—According to Govett, a remarkable rendering is found in some manuscripts: "Because of thy will they were *not*, and were created"; this gives the meaning that whether at first God had *not* created or now God *has* created all things, it is nonetheless all by His will.

5.1–4 "WHO IS WORTHY TO OPEN THE BOOK?"

5.1 "Him that sat on the throne" is God the Father. "A book"—What book is it? It is the New Covenant, since the New Covenant tells how God will save the church, Israel, the world, and the universe.

"Close sealed with seven seals"—All seven seals, not just one seal, must be opened before what has been determined in the book can be seen.

This book is the New Covenant established by the Lamb with His blood. All the plans of God are presented in the New Covenant.

5.2 "A strong angel proclaiming with a great voice"—It takes a strong angel with a loud voice to proclaim what must be heard in heaven, on earth, and under the earth.

"Who is worthy" is not a matter of power, but of qualification. Who is worthy to bring in the plan of God? None is worthy.

5.3 No one in heaven or on the earth is found worthy to loose the seals.

5.4 "And I wept much"—Fearful lest God's plan could not be executed, John wept much. Here is a heart which is in full sympathy with that of the throne.

5.5–7 "LION . . . LAMB"

5.5 "The Lion that is of the tribe of Judah"—Kings proceed from the tribe of Judah. Before God, our Lord is the Lamb and not a lion; but to the Jews He is the Lion of the tribe of Judah. The lion is mighty and kingly.

"The Root of David"—David is the first king after God's heart whom God has chosen. The Lord Jesus is a shoot that comes out of the stock of Jesse; yet He is not a branch of

David but the Root of David; for David is king after the pattern of the Lord Jesus.

God needs a conquering King to open the book and to execute His plan.

5.6 "A Lamb standing"—The scene at the ascension of the Lord.

As we have indicated earlier, "as though it had been slain" should be rendered "as though it had been *newly* slain".

"Having seven horns, and seven eyes"—Horn speaks of power, for there is power in the horns of oxen and sheep. Accordingly, the Bible uses such expressions as "our horn shall be exalted" (Ps. 89.17), and "the horn of my salvation" (Ps. 18.2). Eye represents intelligence. The seven Spirits of God are as torches being sent to the dark world. The seven Spirits of God rest upon the Lord Jesus to give Him power, wisdom, and so forth (Is. 11.2). The seven Spirits cause us to draw nearer to the Lord and to praise Him.

5.7 The Lamb takes the book. The heavens and the earth shall then break forth in praises (see below). The New Covenant is now in the hand of the Lamb and it will soon be implemented.

5.8–10 THE DOXOLOGY OF "THE FOUR LIVING CREATURES AND THE TWENTY-FOUR ELDERS"
5.11–13 LAUDATION OF ANGELS AND ALL CREATED THINGS

5.8 The focus of the prayers of the saints is upon the second coming of the Lord. Harps are for praising and bowls of incense are for presenting prayers.

5.9 "A new song"—Because the Lord has only newly died, therefore it is a new song.

"Every tribe, and tongue, and people, and nation"—Four earthly things are mentioned here, and four is the number of the earth.

"And didst purchase unto God"—Those who are purchased by the blood are not the 24 elders, since it is recorded that they do not sing "didst purchase unto God *us*", but "them".

5.10 According to what has been said here, are not all believers kings and priests? Yes, our salvation is based on the Lord's death, yet it is also through man's faith. Similarly, then, we are made priests and kings to God by the finished work of the Lord's blood, but we actually serve as priests and kings both today and in the kingdom through our faithful dedication.

5.11,12 Includes the angels, the 24 elders, and the four living creatures.

5.13 This is the praise of all the created things in the universe.

PART FOUR

OPENING SEALS

Opening Seals
(6.1–8.5)

Are the six seals in chapter 6 already fulfilled, in the process of being fulfilled, or waiting to be fulfilled in the tribulation to come? There are two evidences to show that these are either fulfilled already or in the process of being fulfilled.

(1) In 5.2 it is declared: "Who is worthy to open the book, and to loose the seals thereof?" But by the time of 5.7 the Lamb has taken the book. Will He thereafter wait two thousand years before He opens the seven seals?

(2) Unless God in His dealing is setting aside the church, He cannot acknowledge He is now dealing with the Jews. Yes, by the time of 7.1–8 God does begin to acknowledge the Jews and to choose them as His servants. But this section in chapter 7 follows upon the sixth seal. It therefore logically indicates that the time before the sixth seal is the time of the church.

From these two evidences we may conclude that the six seals are either already fulfilled or in the process of being fulfilled.

6.1–2 "ONE OF THE SEVEN SEALS . . . A WHITE HORSE"

Why use four living creatures to announce the four horses? Perhaps for the simple reason that there are four horses.

6.2 What is the significance of the white horse? There are three different interpretations.

(1) It refers to Antichrist. The reasons are as follows:

a) Christ does not ride on a white horse till in the time of chapter 19. So that this incident cannot refer to Him.

b) In speaking of the tribulation, Matthew 24 relates four things, among which are mentioned false christs. Naturally, then, what is being referred to here should be the false christ.

c) There being a bow but without an arrow indicates that the victory is not real. Thus this cannot refer to Christ.

(2) It alludes to international peace pacts, and the arguments for this interpretation are as follows:

a) White is the color of righteousness, hence the saints wear white garments and the Lord rides upon a white horse. This is peace brought in through righteousness.

b) A bow without an arrow is a sign of peace. International peace is thus maintained with righteous might.

(3) It points to Christ, and the reasons given for this interpretation are as follows:

a) Since the one who rides the white horse mentioned in chapter 19 is Christ, it naturally must be Christ in chapter 6.

b) Since power and authority rendered to the other three horses are given by God, that of the first horse must also be given by God. And whom will God crown except Christ?

c) Only Christ comes forth conquering and to conquer.

d) Christ must have taken the bow before He was crowned. A bow without an arrow implies that the arrow has already been shot and that thus it has dealt the devil a fatal wound. God therefore crowns Christ that He may be glorified.

e) Concerning the four horses, only in 6.4 is the word "another" used, thus intimating that the first horse is different from the later three horses.

f) The priority in God's plan is that His Son shall conquer—and His conquest is the victory of the gospel. (One of the four living creatures says "Come" [in some old manuscripts it is rendered "Go"], for the living creatures themselves do not speak with the tone of command.)

Which of the three interpretations is correct? The third one (pointing to Christ) seems to be more reasonable, hence we will decide on Christ.

6.3-4 "THE SECOND SEAL . . . A RED HORSE"

Red is the color of blood. Taking peace away means war.

The first horse (white) conquers by the bow, so it is battling at a distance. The red horse fights with a sword, so it is battling in proximity. The phrase "to take peace from the earth" proves that war is for the sake of war, not for the sake of ideology. War that aims at "slay(ing) one another" is considered by the Bible to be the worst kind. It accomplishes nothing but death, destruction, and annihilation (Judges 7.22; Zech. 8.10; Jer. 25.15-31; Lev. 26.25).

6.5-6 "THE THIRD SEAL . . . A BLACK HORSE"

Black is the color for famine (Jer. 14.1-3; Lam. 4.8,9; 5.10). In the Bible, wheat and barley are usually shown as being sold by measure; balances are used to weigh precious things. But a balance is here used for wheat and barley, which indicates that every grain is taken into account.

"A measure of wheat for a shilling"—In Matthew 20.2 we find that the wages for a laborer are one shilling a day. This is therefore the daily wages for one person. So what he earns is just enough for his own consumption.

"And three measures of barley for a shilling"—The difference in value between wheat and barley is normally stated in the ratio of one to two, but at this time it has become a ratio of one to three (see 2 Kings 7.16, 18 for the one-to-two ratio).

"And the oil and the wine hurt thou not"—This hints that oil and wine were wasted in other times since they are not staple food. But now they ought not be wasted for it is the time of famine. Nevertheless, this also suggests that vines and olive trees are being kept by God.

For the past two thousand years war and famine and earthquake have increased in number and scope as well as in intensity and in closer occurrence to each other.

6.7–8 "THE FOURTH SEAL . . . A PALE HORSE"

The word "pale" here is the same Greek word translated "green" in Mark 6.39 and Revelation 8.7 and 9.4. Green is the color of grass. When this color appears on the face it signifies either sickness or death. And hence the name of the one who sits on this pale horse is called Death.

"Hades" is the subterranean, unseen world. Hades here serves as a dustpan into which the dead are swept.

By the sword of the red horse, the famine of the black horse, and the pestilence of the pale horse, plus the wild beasts of the earth, one fourth of the world's population will be killed.

The use of "wild beasts" is one of God's severest judgments (Num. 21.6; 2 Kings 2.24, 17.25).

6.9-11 "THE FIFTH SEAL . . . UNDERNEATH THE ALTAR
THE SOULS . . . CRIED"

The Bible frequently divides the number seven into four
and three or three and four. Three is the number of God,
and four is the number of man. Four followed by three
means that man advances and draws nigh to God. Three
followed by four indicates a falling from a good position to
the lower level of man. Since the churches are seen and
discussed in chapters 2 and 3 as first three and then four,
they are depicted as going downhill. But the seven seals are
mentioned in a cluster of four first and of three next, so that
what is expressed here is different from what is expressed in
the discussion of the seven churches.

What this passage of Scripture speaks of is the situation
of the church being persecuted during these two thousand
years.

6.9 "The word of God" includes all the commandments of God.

"And for the testimony which they held" means that the
believers bear witness to the testimony of the Lord Jesus
habitually (Rev. 1.2, 6.9, 12.17). Some people maintain
that this passage does not refer to the church under
persecution because it has not mentioned that they held to
the testimony of Jesus. Instead, the passage should be
considered as referring to the persecution of the Old
Testament saints. Yet if we remember that the purpose of
this whole book is centered around the testimony of Jesus,
then "the testimony which they held" must be in connection with the same testimony, and therefore it must be the
Lord's children in view here.

"The altar"—The Bible speaks of two altars: (1) that
upon which the sacrifices are offered, and (2) the golden

altar of incense. One renowned writer declared that all the altars in the book of Revelation should be translated as altars of incense. But there is not sufficient justification for such an assertion.

On the contrary, the altar here must be the altar of sacrifices—for the following reasons.

(1) According to Old Testament typology, no one should go up to the altar with his nakedness uncovered (Ex. 20.26). This signifies that no naked body can meet God. Anyone who does not have a resurrection body is considered naked, and therefore he cannot appear before God. For this reason, 2 Corinthians 5.4 speaks about being "clothed upon" with a new body. (After a person is dead, his soul does not go to God right away.) Without resurrection, no one can stand beside the golden altar of incense.

(2) When the Bible speaks of altar, it always refers to the altar of sacrifice. Special descriptive words such as "golden", "incense", and so forth are used to refer to the golden altar of incense so as to distinguish it from the altar standing in the outer court.

(3) The blood of all the sacrifices flows down underneath the altar (Ex. 29.12; Lev. 4.7, 5.9).

(4) There is life in the blood, and this word "life" in the original Hebrew is the word "soul" (Lev. 17.11 mg., 17.14). "Underneath the altar" means underneath the earth. The altar typifies the cross; beneath the cross is the earth. Hence underneath the altar here refers to Paradise in the heart of the earth (Matt. 12.40). We notice the following clause in Acts 2.27: "because thou wilt not leave my soul unto Hades"; moreover, in Numbers 16.32 it is stated that "the earth opened its mouth, and swallowed them up, and their households, and all the men that appertained unto Korah, and all their goods" (Not only may no man appear before

God without a body, neither may he enter the lake of fire without a body.).

"Slain"—During the Roman era, Christians were persecuted and many were slain. The writer of the book of Revelation, John himself, was among the persecuted. Even as recently as in modern Russia, countless numbers of Christians have been killed.

6.10 "O Master, the holy and true"—Govett felt that this was the way the Old Testament saints addressed the Lord, yet in Revelation 3.7 the Lord himself told the church that He is the one who is holy and true. Thus we here find the saints addressing the Lord.

"Them that dwell on the earth"—Such an expression is found many times in this book (8.13; 13.8,12; 13.14; 14.6; 17.2,8). It refers to those who make earth their home and have their all on earth. These will God judge. According to 3.10 the hour of trial will come upon the whole world to try them that dwell upon the earth.

The prayer here is not the same as Stephen's, for Stephen prayed for God's mercy while the prayer in this passage is for judgment. Hence the saints here are praying against sinners.

"Avenge our blood"—God does not forget the prayer of the poor (Ps. 9.12). When God begins to judge those who have persecuted the saints, He avenges His saints.

6.11 "White robe"—This shows that God has justified them because they were accepted by Him. The justification here is different from that of salvation since this is the verdict of God who on the throne is announcing that the saints have won the case, they only waiting for the verdict to be executed.

"Rest yet for a little time"—This word alone may prove that the church cannot be raptured all at once, because this waiting implies a long and protracted persecution.

"Until their fellow-servants also and their brethren"— During the Great Tribulation there will be great slaughter. In 7.13–15 political persecution is spoken of, but 17.6 refers to religious persecution. The way for the church is through death.

The Bible seems to imply that at the first rapture there is no resurrection. The phrase "underneath the altar" does not refer to death as a result of a sin-offering, rather it alludes to death as a consequence of a burnt-offering (Ex. 40.6,10,29; Lev. 4.7,10,18; 1 Chron. 6.49, 16.40, 21.29; 2 Chron. 29.18).

What men take note of is the sin-offering, but that which God sees first is the burnt-offering. Although without the Lord Jesus ever being the sin-offering we would none of us have life, nevertheless God will not accept anything without Christ being the burnt-offering—that is to say, His offering His all to God in obeying and doing God's will. Here do we see that even His death on the cross is according to the will of God. In that same spirit of Christ Paul too offered himself as a burnt-offering (Phil. 2.17; 2 Tim. 4.6). Throughout his life he was a living sacrifice.

All the martyrs shall enter the kingdom to reign. Three classes of people will reign with Christ (20.4): (1) "thrones, and they sat upon them"—this refers to those people such as are cited in 3.21; (2) "them that had been beheaded for the testimony of Jesus, and for the word of God" (they are now resurrected)—here it is a reference to those people as are found mentioned in 6.11; and (3) "such as worshipped not the beast, neither his image"—this is referring to those fellow-servants and their brethren mentioned in 6.11 (they also are resurrected).

6.12–17 "THE SIXTH SEAL . . . A GREAT EARTHQUAKE"

The Bible gives two accounts in Joel and Matthew of the celestial cataclysm and earthquake that are to occur at the second coming of the Lord. One cataclysmic event will occur in advance of the day of His coming and another one will follow the day of His return. In other words, one will happen before the Great Tribulation and another will occur after the Great Tribulation. Joel 3.16–17 and 2.30–31 describe what will happen before the great and terrible day of the Lord, that is, in advance of the Great Tribulation. On the other hand, Matthew 24.29–30 explains what will come to pass after these days of the Great Tribulation are over. Therefore, the sixth seal speaks of the situation prior to the Great Tribulation.

6.12–14 We dare not say this section has all been fulfilled, but neither dare we state that none of it has been fulfilled. A century ago some similar scenes happened in Australia, with people at that time manifesting the conditions as described in 6.15–16. Thus, what is given in this section seems to have been fulfilled. However, what is depicted in 6.14 has never been witnessed in history with such intensity, and therefore it waits to be fulfilled.

"Black as sackcloth of hair"—The tent used by the Jews as well as by the Arabs is made of black sackcloth, hence such a description.

"The stars of the heaven fell unto the earth"—(1) These stars may refer to meteors; and (2) Since some stars are far bigger than the earth, how can they fall upon the earth? Most likely they are to fall in a direction *towards* the earth rather than fall *upon* the earth.

6.15–16 This passage reveals the working of their

conscience. They are conscious of the coming of God's judgment. Only the blood of our Lord can give peace to our conscience and cause us to escape the wrath of God. How much more dependable the Blood is than the mountains and the rocks.

The Visions Interposed Between the Sixth Seal and the Seventh Seal

7.1–8 THE REMNANT OF THE CHILDREN OF ISRAEL

God has two classes of people as His own possession: the earthly Jewish people, and the spiritual church. This section speaks of the earthly Jewish people, among whom a number will be kept by God; but the next section (7.9–17) alludes to the situation in heaven after the church is raptured.

According to strict Biblical presentation, the Great Tribulation lasts only three years and a half; the rest is either tribulation or trial. (Possibly the fifth trumpet is the beginning of the Great Tribulation.)

7.1 "Winds"—Many times in the Old Testament "wind" stands for God's judgment. For instance, in Jonah's time there came forth a great wind and a mighty tempest on the sea (Jonah 1.13; see also Is. 11.15; Jer. 13.24, 22.22, 49.36, 51.1). Moreover, the phrase "the winds blew", recorded in Matthew 7.25, refers to a kind of trial.

"No wind should blow on the earth, or on the sea, or upon any tree"—Thus is there calm on the earth, with not a wave on the sea nor a sound among the trees. For God is purposed to seal those whom He will preserve. At the opening of the seventh seal there will come forth the seven trumpets. And at the sounding of the first trumpet one third of the sea will turn to blood.

7.2 "Another angel"—Who is this angel? The word "angel" here is "messenger" in the original Greek. The angels are sometimes called messengers, but so too are men sometimes designated this. In this book, the special designation "another angel" is used several times. The word "another" indicates its difference from the rest (8.3, 10.1–3, 18.1). Now in all these places, who else but the Lord Jesus has such majesty and honor? D. M. Panton has remarked that the word "another" is very meaningful for it signifies another class or another kind.

"The Angel of the Lord" in the Old Testament is a specific title (Gen. 16.7–14, 22.1–13, 32.24–30; Judges 13.16–18) which is always a reference to the Lord Jesus.

The Lord is here called an "angel"—which is an Old Testament denomination—thus hinting that He will soon return to His Old Testament ground.

7.3 "The servants of our God"—God begins to recognize the Jews, inasmuch as He is going to return to the position He held in the Old Testament. (During the church age there is no distinction between the Jews and the Gentiles.) Since this book centers on the throne of God the people are called servants, for they are placed in a position of responsibility rather than in that of children.

"Another angel . . . having the seal of the living God"—This seal must be put in the hand of God's most trusted one. Besides God the Father the Lord Jesus is the first and foremost Person. As Pharaoh placed his seal in the hand of Joseph, so God put His seal in the hand of the Lord Jesus.

"And he cried . . . to the four angels to whom it was given"—All that is to come upon the earth comes from God, for without His giving anyone authority none can do anything.

Note that 7.1–3 tells of the winds, and 8.6–9, of the fire. Wind and fire are most intimately related. After a tempestuous wind there comes a raging fire.

7.4–8 Who are these people?

(1) Not the church.

The Seventh Day Adventists consider themselves this people because they keep the law and hence they are the true Jews. But there are ten reasons to prove that the people in this passage are the Jews according to the flesh.

(a) If "the children of Israel" spoken of in 2.14 is to be explained literally, then "the children of Israel" found in 7.4 must also be literally interpreted.

(b) Since "the tribe of Judah" mentioned in 5.5 is literal, so must "the tribe of Judah" mentioned in 7.5 be literal.

(c) The names of the twelve tribes belong only to the children of Israel; who can therefore say which Christian denomination comes under the name of which tribe of Israel?

(d) Israel has twelve tribes, but the church is one. How can the church be divided into twelve tribes?

(e) 7.9 speaks of "every nation", so "Israel" spoken of in 7.4 must be a nation.

(f) The great multitude told of in 7.9 is numberless, while those mentioned in 7.3–4 who receive the seal on their foreheads are numbered as 144,000. How can anyone restrict the saved ones of the church to a group numbering only 144,000? Furthermore, this number of 144,000 is made up of 12 twelve thousands. It would thus be unreasonable not to interpret literally.

(g) "The kings" spoken of in 6.15 are taken literally; how then can "Israel" found in 7.4 not be reckoned as a nation?

(h) Because John did not know where this great multitude came from, he said to one of the elders, "Thou knowest" (7.13,14). Yet he did not ask about those told of in 7.4 8, since evidently he had already known who they were.

(i) In Joel 2.2–27 we read that God only tells Israel how to escape the locusts, and in Revelation 9.3,4 we read that only those whom God has sealed escape the hurt of the locusts. It is thus proven beyond doubt that the sealed are the Jews.

(j) The sheep mentioned in Matthew 25 treat well the little brother ("one of these my brethren, even these least"—v.40). (This little brother points to the Jews or those Christians who yet remain on earth.) This little brother—Israel—will become the test for the nations in the future.

(2) Not the church but the various people of Israel.

Before we deal with this group in general let us first notice that in 7.4–8 no name of Dan is mentioned. According to Ezekiel chapters 40–48 which predict the situation concerning the future kingdom, Dan will be located at the north end (48.1). Why then is Dan not mentioned here? This does not mean that Dan as a tribe has disappeared; it may suggest, though, the close relationship Dan has with the serpent. We will recall that as Jacob prophesied over his sons he mentioned Dan (Gen. 49.16–18). Verse 16 of that passage told of Dan's existence and verse 17 of his conduct; but in verse 18 Jacob suddenly bursts out in prayer. He had not done this when prophesying concerning his other sons. Probably Dan's behavior in the future would be highly dangerous. During the Great Tribulation the tribe of Dan may join itself to Antichrist in some special relationship.

These people who are sealed with the seal of the living God are:

a) the Jews who will rule with Christ on earth in the

future (though not as kings). Twelve thousand is the resultant number of the multiples of 12, it being 12 x 10^3. This number represents the eternal perfection of God's government.

b) the suffering Jews who make up part of the little brother mentioned in Matthew 25.

c) the Jewish counterpart of those who endure to the end as spoken of in Matthew 24.

d) the Jews upon whom the Holy Spirit will be poured out in the coming day (the former rain has already been poured out—Acts 2, but the latter rain is yet to be poured forth—Joel 2.28–29). The blood and fire mentioned in Joel 2.30 coincide with the phenomena of the first trumpet; the pillars of smoke agree with the fifth trumpet. Thus the second outpouring of the Holy Spirit will occur between the sixth seal and the fifth trumpet.

And e) those Jews who receive the New Covenant when the Lord Jesus shall establish His New Covenant with Israel on earth (Jer. 31.31–34).

7.9-17 THE SCENE IN HEAVEN
AFTER THE CHURCH IS RAPTURED

This section sketches for us this scene in heaven. Who is the great multitude? Though we dare not conclude definitely that this refers to the whole church, we would nevertheless say that it includes the majority of the redeemed of God; that is, it consists of those in the first rapture, plus that great number who are raised from the dead, together with the relatively smaller number of those who yet remain alive on earth and are changed. Here we are not shown how the church is raptured, only an outline description is given of the heavenly scene after the church has been raptured. Yet how do we know that this is the scene in heaven of the raptured church? The reasons are given below.

(1) The number: "a great multitude, which no man could number" (7.9). At the first rapture there cannot be such a vast number. Hence this must be a conglomeration of several raptures.

(2) "Standing before the throne and before the Lamb"— Since 4.2 reads that "there was a throne set *in heaven*", those who now stand before the throne here must have arrived in heaven.

(3) The great tribulation spoken of in 7.14 is the same as mentioned in John 16.33. Therefore, the countless number here includes all who have been persecuted throughout the centuries: some have gone through martyrdom, many have been raised from the dead. Those who are resurrected will naturally surpass in number those at the first rapture.

Please note that 7.9-17 narrates the period from the rapture (the first rapture) to eternity (the new heaven and the new earth). What is described in 7.15-17 depicts the same scene as is found in 21.3-7.

Note also that 7.9-17 only deals with rapture generally, not exclusively; and neither does it speak exclusively of the scene of eternal blessing. Consequently, we must not conclude that what is given here is indicative of the rapture of the whole church once and for all; for nothing is said as to how this vast multitude got there, it only states that they are there.

7.9 "After these things . . . , standing before the throne and before the Lamb"—This word implies that before the opening of the seventh seal there must be a rapture.

Who is the great multitude? They are the redeemed ones by the precious blood of the Lord during these past two thousand years. The positive arguments for this view are as follows.

(1) The number. "And behold, a great multitude, which no man could number"—Those who belong to Israel are usually numbered in the Scriptures, such, for example, as the twelve tribes, the seventy souls which went down into Egypt, and the certain number of people given as coming up out of Egypt. We also have the various numberings recorded in the book of Numbers; we in addition see how David numbered his people. It seems that generation after generation the number belonging to Israel was continually given.

Even as is indicated in 7.1–8, they have a number. Although in the church there is first the 12 apostles, then the 70, and later the 120, the 3,000, and the 5,000, it is also stated that "the Lord added to them day by day those that were saved" (Acts 2.47). But here in 7.9 it is declared that "no man could number" the multitude.

By doing a little arithmetic we will readily see that this great multitude cannot be the people who will come out of the three and a half years' Great Tribulation. For the biggest number recorded in this book of Revelation is twice ten thousand times ten thousand, which amounts to 200 millions. Now in order to be that which no man could number, this multitude needs to be a number greater than the 200 millions comprising the armies of the horsemen (9.16).

(2) Whence. "Out of every nation and of all tribes and peoples and tongues" (7.9)—With respect to 5.9–10, we know these who come out of every nation and tribe and people and tongue are the Gentiles chosen and gathered to God. In other words, the church. ("God visited the Gentiles, to take out of them a people for his name", Acts 15.14–19. During the church age, even a Jew is saved after the

manner of the Gentile, that is, he takes the position of the Gentile while he believes in the Lord. Hence the church may be considered to be the saved among the Gentiles. Unquestionably, in the church there is neither Jew nor Gentile.)

(3) Whereto. In 6.17 the question is asked—"Who is able to stand?"; here in 7.9–17 are a people who have arrived and stand before God. Only to the church has God given the promise of rapture, and none but the church may stand before God.

(4) When will God return to deal with the Jews? Not "until the fulness of the Gentiles be come in" (Rom. 11.25,26). Therefore, the multitude here must be the people referred to in Romans 11.25. It is the church.

(5) To none of the 24 elders, the four living creatures, and the 144,000 is it said that they are purchased with the blood; but to this people here it is stated that they are washed in the blood.

(6) Though they are arrayed in white robes which is God's promise to the church in Sardis, yet Sardis and Philadelphia cannot have included such a tremendously large number of people. Who else except the church possesses such a glorious future? Hence what is depicted here must be the scene of the raptured of the church in heaven.

(7) The attitude of the angels. The first word uttered by the angels is "Amen" (7.12). There is joy over the sinner who repents (Luke 15.7). How can the angels refrain from rejoicing and praising when they see so many people coming before the throne and before the Lamb?

(8) Their robes are made white by being washed in the blood (7.14). This is the unique privilege of the church.

(9) 7.15–17 is quite similar to the situation in eternity as given in 21.3–7. The overcoming mentioned in 21.7 is the

faith that overcomes (1 John 5.4), for the previous verse reads: "I will give unto him that is athirst of the fountain of the water of life freely" (21.6).

"Arrayed in white robes" (7.9)—This refers to the cleanness of conduct, because the robes are washed white in the blood (7.14).

"And palms in their hands"—This signifies victory (Lev. 23.39–43). During the feast of tabernacles branches of palm trees are used, which feast denotes that God will temporarily dwell with His people (thus typifying the millennial kingdom).

7.14 The phrase "the great tribulation" is not the Great Tribulation of three years and a half duration. The reasons are as follows.

(1) At the earliest, the Great Tribulation should commence at the sounding of the "woe" trumpets, the first of which is the fifth (8.13, 9.1a). Yet 7.9 is an intimation of a rapture having taken place before the seventh seal. Some of these people must have arrived at the throne without passing through the time of the "woe" trumpets.

(2) The Great Tribulation cannot begin before Satan is cast down to earth. Satan will be cast down at the sounding of the fifth trumpet (9.1); and before the horrible situation of the 42 months prevails on earth (13.5), the man child is already raptured to the throne (12.5). Though this man child may not include all the people referred to in 7.9, nonetheless we dare say that it embraces a part of that great multitude.

(3) As soon as the seventh bowl is poured, the kingdom arrives. During the kingdom age we do not see the temple in heaven, instead we see the temple on earth as described in Ezekiel. Who will have the time and opportunity to serve

God during the Great Tribulation? Yet 7.15 clearly states that God's servants serve Him day and night.

(4) There cannot be so many people saved at the Great Tribulation. Since the great multitude mentioned in 7.9 is said to have come out of the great tribulation (7.14), *this* great tribulation must be different from that which comes at the fifth and sixth trumpets.

(5) According to 11.1, there are those who worship in the temple of God in heaven. Aside from the people cited in 7.9, where can there be found any who worship God in heaven? For at that time the Great Tribulation as predicted in the book of Revelation has yet to begin. In the new heaven and the new earth, no temple is seen (21.22) because the Lord God the Almighty and the Lamb are the temple thereof. (God and the Lamb form the center of the new city. Following the mentioning of the temple of God in 3.12 are found the words "he shall go out thence no more", for the simple reason that God and the Lamb are the temple in the new heaven and the new earth.)

(6) The Bible expressly says that there are believers who do not pass through the Great Tribulation (for example, Luke 21.36 and Rev. 3.10).

(7) Suppose these people mentioned in 7.9 did in fact pass through the Great Tribulation of three and a half years; then they must have died at the time when the temple is trodden underfoot by the nations. But according to what is given in 11.2 it is impossible to include the church therein. So how can it be held that the multitude cited in 7.9 comes out of the Great Tribulation of three and a half years?

(8) The Great Tribulation of three years and a half spoken of in Revelation is especially related to the Jews. Both Daniel 12.1—"And there shall be a time of trouble,

such as never was since there was a nation even to that same time: and at that time thy people shall be delivered . . ."—and Matthew 24.16–18 depict particularly the situation of the Jewish people. God's primary purpose is to make use of the Great Tribulation to deal with the Jews. "The time of Jacob's trouble" spoken of in Jeremiah 30.7 manifestly points to the Jews. But in the book of Revelation reference is made to the subject of tribulation several times in connection with the church, such as in 1.9 and 2.9–10,13. According to John 16.33 tribulation seems to be the earthly portion of the church for she must pass through a prolonged duration of sufferings. Accordingly, this tribulation may also be described in the same way as Revelation 7.14 itself *literally* does in the Greek original, namely: "the tribulation the great". Nevertheless, the great tribulation cited in Revelation 2.22 is very different from that in 7.14, nor is it the same as that of the three and a half years mentioned elsewhere in Revelation. (The words "through many tribulations we must enter into the kingdom of God" in Acts 14.22 has reference to the common experience those who enter the kingdom of God will share on earth.)

"And they washed their robes, and made them white in the blood of the Lamb" (7.14b). "Robes" is in plural number, and these robes signify righteousnesses, even the righteousnesses of the saints. They do not refer to the Lord Jesus Christ as our righteousness. Indeed, the robe (singular) is righteousness (Is. 61.10), and it is the Lord himself (Jer. 23.6), for Christ is our righteousness (1 Cor. 1.30). We are clothed with Him as we come before God. But this righteousness has no need to be cleansed by the blood.

Hence we have two robes: the one we are clothed with when we are saved, by which we stand before God; the other is our own righteousnesses—even our victories—in which we may stand before Christ. The white garments spoken of in Revelation 3.18 require a price, whereas redemption is that which need not be bought.

No Christian will be judged and condemned before God (John 5.24); but no Christian will be exempt from having to stand and be judged before the judgment seat of Christ according to what he has done (2 Cor. 5.10).

Believers' robes are washed clean, yet not because of the great tribulation but because of the blood of the Lamb.

The very fact that the robes of the saints are washed in the blood of the Lamb shows how they once were defiled on earth yet they have followed the instruction of 1 John 1.9, and thus they are cleansed.

7.15 "Therefore"—This is a continuation of what has been mentioned before. They are qualified to serve God because they do not overlook sins.

7.16–17 Compare these two verses with Isaiah 49.10 (also cf. Is. 49.6 with Acts 13.47; Is. 49.8 with 2 Cor. 6.2).

"Hunger no more, neither thirst any more"—These words show how all expectations have been satisfied.

"Neither shall the sun strike upon them, nor any heat"—In the holy city, the New Jerusalem, there is no need of the sun or of the moon (21.23, 22.5). Not that there is no more sun nor moon, but that there is *no need* of these lights. On the new earth however, there will still be night, for since day is mentioned in Revelation 21.25, there must also still be night on the new earth.

"Wipe away every tear from their eyes"—This reveals that there will now be no need to shed tears.

The multitude mentioned in 7.9–17 and the people represented by the man child in 12.1–11 have many points in common:

(1) According to 7.10 the multitude are saved by the Lamb, and according to 12.11 those included in the man child overcome because of the blood of the Lamb.

(2) Those mentioned in 7.9 stand before the throne; the man child spoken of in 12.5 is raptured to the throne.

(3) Salvation is attributed to God and to the Lamb in 7.10, and in 12.10 salvation is said to come from God and His Christ.

(4) We read in 7.1-8 that the twelve tribes are sealed, and we read in 12.1 that the woman has upon her head a crown of twelve stars. (The crown of twelve stars does not refer to the twelve apostles, for Joseph dreamed of twelve stars and those clearly pointed to the twelve tribes.)

(5) We find in 7.11 that the angels burst out in praises, and we find in 12.10 that a great voice is heard in heaven.

(6) Since the people spoken of in 7.9 stand before the throne of God they must have resurrection bodies, and likewise the man child spoken of in 12.5 must have a resurrection body. The word "delivered" in verse 5 should be explained according to the rule of interpreting visions, not according to the rule of literal interpretation. From the explanation given in Acts 13.33-34, we can readily see that this is resurrection. Without a resurrection body no one can see God, for he will be reckoned as naked (2 Cor. 5.2,3; Ex. 20.26, 28.42). 1 Corinthians 15 speaks of resurrection as a sure fact; 2 Corinthians 5 speaks of the facts about resurrection. Today there is no Christian before the throne; this will be true later in the future. In Revelation 4.6 no one is shown standing on the glassy sea; only by the time of Revelation 15 will there be people standing on it (v.2 mg.). Acts 2.34 explicitly says that David has not ascended to heaven, and 1 Samuel 28.13-14 definitely states that Samuel came up out of the earth. Both indicate that they have not yet been clothed with a resurrection body. The

Lord alone is one who descended out of heaven and yet is in heaven (John 3.13). Even Enoch and Elijah, who were taken to heaven, may presently be placed somewhere else, since they probably do not have a transformed body.

(7) In 7.15 we have the words "spread his tabernacle over them", in 12.12 we have the words "O heavens, and ye that dwell in them" which in Greek is "ye that tabernacle in them" (see also John 1.14 where "dwelt" in Greek is actually "tabernacled").

(8) Those mentioned in 7.9 are overcomers, for (a) the white garments are promised to those in Sardis who have not defiled their garments, (b) not to pass through the trial of the Great Tribulation to come is assured to those in Philadelphia who have kept the word of patience, and (c) the palm is always a symbol of victory. The man child spoken of in 12.5 is likewise an overcomer, since he will rule the nations with a rod of iron.

[Here end the visions interposed between the sixth and seventh seals.]

TRUMPETS, SEALS, AND BOWLS

Seals are opened secretly, trumpets are sounded openly. In the Old Testament, the blowing of a trumpet was something solemn. It is equally so here (note that 1.10 and 4.1 are only rendered: "*as* of a trumpet").

Out of the seventh seal come the seven trumpets, and out of the seventh trumpet issue forth the seven bowls. The seven trumpets succeed one another in order, and each covers a prolonged period—such as is the case in the fifth trumpet, where 9.10 describes it as being five months; in the case of the sixth trumpet 9.15 shows it to be at least thirteen months ("hour and day and month and year"); and in the seventh trumpet 10.7 mentions "the days of the voice of the seventh angel". According to 11.15, at the end of the seventh trumpet the kingdom of God shall come. But the seventh trumpet includes seven bowls, that is to say, the seven bowls are equal in time to the seventh trumpet. It is therefore different from the seven trumpets which come out of the seventh seal in that the trumpets have extended durations while there is not much time after the blowing of the seventh trumpet.

To better understand this we may draw a diagram as follows:

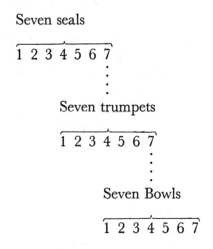

Seven seals

1 2 3 4 5 6 7

Seven trumpets

1 2 3 4 5 6 7

Seven Bowls

1 2 3 4 5 6 7

It takes approximately two thousand years to open the seals. Not till the seventh seal is opened can the contents of the book be seen. As the seventh seal includes seven trumpets, the writings in the book will still remain hidden even after the blowing of the sixth trumpet. It awaits the sounding of the seventh trumpet to have the book completely opened. As soon as the seventh trumpet is blown, the kingdom is ushered in. Then shall the New Covenant be seen—the blessings which God has prepared for the earth (Jer. 31.31–34, 33.14–15).

Both the seals and the trumpets are of extended duration. The difference between them lies in the fact that the seals will hurt the fourth part of the earth (6.8), whereas the trumpets will hurt the third part of the earth (8.7).

The seventh trumpet commences with the first bowl and ends with the seventh bowl. This agrees with Romans 16.25,26. Revelation 11.15 refers to the end of the seventh trumpet, hence the kingdom immediately arrives.

By comparing "thy wrath" in 11.15–18 with "the wrath of God" in 15.1 we can see that the seven bowls constitute the wrath of God.

The opening of the seals is done in heaven in secret; the blowing of the trumpets is meant as proclamations to the earth for all to hear; and the pouring of the bowls reveals their contents without making any noise. The opening of the seals speaks of judgments during the gospel age such as famine, earthquake, war, and so forth, of which the world does not know their origin—only the believers know, hence it is secretive. The blowing of the trumpets indicates that the dispensation is changed, for the gospel age has come to an end. At the time of chapter 7 the children of Israel are sealed and the overcoming believers are raptured, and therefore by the time of chapter 8 comes the declaration of war. A trumpet has the nature of serving notice, and the bowl signifies wrath. We find the *cup* of wrath in the Old Testament, but here it is the *bowls* of wrath—which are obviously much more severe than any cup of wrath.

The tribulations of the seven trumpets are *real* afflictions. Please consider the following observations:

(1) This book of Revelation is not, in the first instance, a book of symbols.

(2) The blowing of trumpets is not a secretive action;

rather, it is something to be heard. Whatever is sounded is what will come to pass. (At the blowing of the last trumpet there will be resurrection. This is truly miraculous just as all the other trumpets are.)

(3) What the seven trumpets proclaim to mankind is the judgment of God.

(4) Since all the Old Testament prophecies—whether they speak of judgment or the Lord's coming—are to be interpreted literally, why should not the prophecies in the New Testament also be explained literally? As the ten plagues of Egypt are literal, why should not the tribulations in Revelation also be literally accepted?

(5) The church age having passed (this being seen in chapter 7), God is now returned to His Old Testament position. Naturally, all the judgments must be taken literally (Micah 7.15). Isaiah 11.15–16 tells how God will once more execute judgment on the nations: "like as there was for Israel in the day that he [Israel] came up out of the land of Egypt", only this time it will be a far greater judgment. Jeremiah 23.7,8 prophesies of a deliverance greater than that of bringing the children of Israel out of the land of Egypt.

(6) The full and final fulfillment of "marvels" spoken of in Exodus 34.10 must be found here at the time of the blowing of trumpets.

(7) All the plagues mentioned in Deuteronomy 28.59 are viewed as "wonderful" (or extraordinary); God's judgments are indeed often miraculous.

(8) The Lord says that the days of the Son of man are like the days of Noah and the days of Lot (Luke 17.26,28). At the time of Noah, God opened the windows of heaven to pour down rain; and in the time of Lot, God rained down brimstone and fire out of heaven. All these are supernatural judgments.

(9) God needs to demonstrate to men that He is Jehovah. Concerning many other afflictions men will attribute them to the change in nature. But for water to turn to blood and only the third part of water to be so turned is evidently not due to the change in nature but is clearly an act of God. When the iniquity of mankind is full, God will judge.

The great tribulation described in Matthew 24.21–28 is especially related to the children of Israel. During that time Antichrist will greatly persecute them. At the earliest, this will commence with the fifth trumpet (9.1–11) and continue on to the seventh trumpet.

The trial told about in Revelation 3.10 is to come upon the whole world, but the great tribulation spoken of in Matthew 24.21–28 is to descend on the Jews. The first one begins at the blowing of the first trumpet, the second commences, at the earliest, from the fifth trumpet.

8.1–2 "THE SEVENTH SEAL . . . A SILENCE"

8.1 At the opening of the seventh seal, there is a silence in heaven. The whole universe grows still, because the time is changing.

8.2 The angels stand, but the 24 elders sit. These seven angels are specially designated as "the seven angels that stand before God"; consequently, some people deem Gabriel to be one of these angels.

Trumpets are designed for war (1 Cor. 14.8; Amos 3.6; Ex. 19.16).

The will of heaven is about ready for blowing, but God is waiting for one thing to be done before He will give the order to blow. That one thing is: the sons of God expressing full accord with God. What He is waiting for is the thing described in 8.3–5. Prayer is the rail to God's will.

8.3–5 SITUATION IN HEAVEN
AFTER OPENING OF SEVEN SEALS

8.3 "And another angel"—This "another angel" is a priest, hence he must be the Lord Jesus. The prayers of all the saints ascend to God through the incense offered by this angel. No Christian can offer up prayer except by means of incense, which signifies the merits of Christ. Through the sweet savor of Christ a believer's prayer reaches before God.

Why is the Lord called an "angel" and not a priest here? Hebrews states: "For verily not to angels doth he [Christ] give help" (2.16). When the New Testament epistles mention the Lord's relationship with us they always describe Him as man. "Wherefore it behooved him in all things to be made like unto his brethren" (Heb. 2.17). Because He is man, therefore He is closer to mankind. The angels are made a little higher than men. In Genesis 18.2,16, and 22 the word "men" is used to show their closeness to Abraham. Genesis 19.1 uses the word "angels" to distinguish them from ordinary men; yet in Genesis 19.10,12, and 16 the word "men" is used again for they were helping Lot. The reason why in Revelation 8.3 the Lord is designated as an angel is to indicate the changing of time. He is no longer the Son of man in the gospel age. He has now become another angel though still a priest.

The saints here are plainly in trials.

In the Old Testament period incense must be burned with the fire on the altar. No strange fire is allowed. Since the altar typifies the cross of our Lord and incense represents prayer, our prayers can reach God only through the merits of our Lord in the redemption accomplished on the cross. Prayer should not be offered with strange fire, that is, with fire not taken from the altar. Without the cross there can be no prayer.

8.4 "The smoke of the incense"—The incense is already lighted. The smoke of the incense speaks of the merits of our Lord. Only smoke may ascend. Except for the Lord's incense, no prayer will reach God's presence.

8.5 "And there followed . . ."—This shows that God has answered the prayers of the saints. Although we do not know what they say in their prayers, we nonetheless know what they pray for through the answer they get. The prayers of the saints here are in accord with the voice underneath the altar in the fifth seal. They are prayers for vengeance (see Luke 18.1–8).

"And the angel taketh the censer; and he filled it with the fire of the altar, and cast it upon the earth"—The answer comes down to where the prayers originated. What is cast on earth is the judgment of God.

PART FIVE

SOUNDING SEVEN TRUMPETS

Sounding Seven Trumpets
(8.6–11.19)

8.6 The seven angels prepare themselves to sound the trumpets.

8.7 God's judgment proceeds from the furtherest place until it strikes men. His judgment falls on other things first, He still expecting repentance from men.

At the sounding of the first trumpet fire is cast upon the earth, consuming the third part of the trees as fuel. In the Old Testament age, soon after the sacrifice was offered by fire the blood was poured out. Hence we have here fire and blood. This fire will burn through the bottomless pit.

And the third part of the trees along with all green grass are burned up. The beauty of nature is first destroyed.

The plague of this trumpet causes the maritime world to lose one third of its business (cf. "the mountains be shaken into the heart of the seas", Ps. 46.2). This trumpet hurts the salty waters.

As both the first and second trumpets use fire, so fire is used in the third trumpet. In remembrance of His covenant with Noah, God will not use water to destroy the earth again (Gen. 9.13–15). "Wormwood" means "bitter" (see Jer. 9.13–15, 23.14–15; Lam. 3.15). This trumpet strikes the non-salty waters.

8.12 "THE FOURTH TRUMPET"

The lights of the sun, moon, and stars, together with the other celestial phenomena, are disturbed; and the world becomes darker. God has not smitten the sun, moon, and stars completely because He remembers His own word (Gen. 8.22).

The plagues of the seals are general, but the plagues of the trumpets are specific and designated. Hence the seals have been and are being fulfilled, while in our time none of the trumpets has as yet been blown.

8.13 Just as the seals are divided into four and three, so the trumpets are divided into four and three. The first four trumpets are merely tribulations, but the last three are the trumpets of woes (9.12, 11.14). The plagues of the first four trumpets are not directed against men; they only affect mankind indirectly. The death of the last three trumpets, however, do come directly to men.

The "eagle" mentioned here is indeed an eagle, for did not the ass of Balaam also speak?

"Them that dwell on the earth"—They are differentiated from those who are mere strangers and sojourners on earth.

9.1–12 "THE FIFTH [TRUMPET] . . . THE FIRST WOE"

The Great Tribulation probably begins at the fifth trumpet since this is a trumpet of woe.

9.1 ". . . a star"—This star cannot be interpreted as a literal star as is the case with the star mentioned in 8.10, because the star here is able to receive the key to the pit of the abyss and to open it. Who is this star? None but Satan himself.

"From heaven fallen unto the earth"—The word "fallen" in the original is the same as the phrase "cast down" in 12.9. "Star" in the Scriptures has reference to angel. In Job we find this verse: "When the morning stars sang together, and all the sons of God shouted for joy" (38.7). Here in Job we are definitely told that the stars stand for the angels in heaven.

Being cast down, this angel cannot be a good one, although as we learn from the apostle he often disguises himself as an angel of light to deceive men (2 Cor. 11.14).

The three and a half years mentioned at various places in the book of Revelation begin and end at the same time. Chapters 11.2–3, 12.6–14, and 13.5 are all simultaneous. The casting down of the star happens at the fifth trumpet, which in turn marks the beginning of the 42 months (the Great Tribulation).

9.2 The bottomless pit is "the pit of the abyss"— What is it? Where is it? It is the habitation of the devil. Luke 8.28,31 tells us that it is the place where demons are tormented. Wherever there is a demon there will be torment there. The demons are in this world, thus making it a demonic world.

The casting down of the star coincides with the record of Luke 10.18. In Luke is the verdict, but here is the execution. When Satan is restricted the pit is closed.

Having smoke simply proves that there is fire within. It is hard to imagine how the pit is opened. The words of Deuteronomy 29.23—"The whole land thereof is brimstone, and salt, and a burning, that it is not sown, nor beareth, nor any grass groweth therein, like the overthrow of Sodom and Gomorrah, Admah and Zeboiim, which Jehovah overthrew in his anger, and in his wrath"—seem like a prophecy of 9.2. For more on smoke, see also Revelation 18.8–9, and 19.3.

From 8.12 we learned that the light in the sky is dimmed by one third of its original brightness, but now the sun and the air are darkened completely here. First, the diminishing of the lights of the sun, moon and stars. Next, their remaining brightness is all covered by smoke.

9.3 "Locusts"—These are not ordinary locusts for the following reasons:

(1) According to 9.4 these locusts, unlike ordinary ones, do not hurt the grass, herbs and trees of the earth but men instead.

(2) The power of these locusts is like that of scorpions (9.3), and they strike men with the torment of a scorpion (9.5). Even their likeness is peculiar (9.7–10), it being totally different from common locusts.

(3) It is stated in Exodus that "neither after them shall [there] be such" (10.14).

(4) From Proverbs 30.27 we read that "the locusts have no king"; yet the locusts here do have a king (9.11).

(5) These locusts come out of the pit of the abyss which is not an ordinary dwelling place; it is the place of the devil.

What are these locusts? Probably they are a special specie possessed by the demons. In this connection please consider the following:

In 9.3,5,7, and 10, it is said of these locusts that they have power as of the scorpions of the earth and their shapes are like horses prepared for war, with tails like scorpions and stings. Combine this information with the fact that the horses in the sixth trumpet have tails like serpents (9.19), and then compare all of this with Luke 10.17–19 where we read that the Lord gives authority to His own to tread upon serpents and scorpions. The cross of our Lord has sentenced Satan to be cast out, and here in 9.1 is the execution of that sentence.

The earth is given to men for habitation, but the pit of the abyss is the place for the devil to dwell.

The word "deep" in Genesis 1.2, according to the Septuagint, is the same word as for the pit of the abyss. It is the dwelling place of the demonic forces. When God divided the waters (Gen. 1.7,8) some of these spiritual hosts of wickedness hovered in the air, thus making it another dwelling place (Eph. 6.12). The sea is probably the mouth to the pit of the abyss. For just as death and Hades give up the dead that are in them, so also the sea gives up the dead that are in it (Rev. 20.13).

The Lord Jesus once descended into the abyss (Rom. 10.7).

9.4,5 These locusts evidently possess supernatural intelligence since they not only can receive orders but also can organize whom God has sealed. (The sealing on the forehead mentioned in 7.1–8 must be a kind of secret sign.)

God orders them not to hurt those men who have the seal of God on their foreheads; and He merely permits them to hurt, but not kill, those without the seal of God on their foreheads.

On the scorpion's tail is a sting which is sharp and cutting, with poison in it. When it strikes, it injects its poison into man and torments him for five months. The severity of an infliction by a scorpion is proverbial (for example, see 2 Chron. 10.11).

9.6 The desire to die is a matter of the heart,

whereas the seeking of death is a question of way. Presently it is death that seeks man, but in the future it will be man seeking death. Men would rather seek death than repent of their sins.

9.7–10 The likenesses of these locusts especially resemble war horses, having golden crowns and breastplates. The breastplates are for their own protection, thus indicating that people will no doubt put up some resistance.

9.11 The king over these locusts is Antichrist. The fallen star mentioned in 9.1 is Satan himself. The beast comes out of the abyss (11.7) or the sea (13.1), suggesting thereby that the abyss is at the bottom of the sea.

"Abaddon" is the name of a place (see Prov. 15.11, 27.20; Job 26.6). In some Scripture passages the word translated "destruction" in some versions is really the word "Abaddon" in the original Hebrew.

The Greek word "Apollyon" is the name of a person. It means Destroyer (see Jer. 4.7, 6.26; Is. 16.4; Dan. 8.24–25, 9.26, 11.44). This messenger of the abyss is therefore named according to his origin and conduct.

9.12 In this first woe, pay special attention to two things: (1) that Satan is cast out of heaven, and (2) that Antichrist comes out of the abyss. And by this time both have now appeared on earth, and their reign shall therefore begin.

9.13–21 with 11.14a   "THE SIXTH [TRUMPET]
. . . THE SECOND WOE"

9.13 "A voice from the horns of the golden altar which is before God"—Some interpret this to be God answering the prayers of the saints. Such an interpretation is faulty, however, because (1) God's answer to prayer should happen at the blowing of the first trumpet since the prayers of the saints are offered with incense on the golden altar as recorded in 8.3; and (2) the voice does not come from the golden altar but comes from *the four horns* of the golden altar. If this indeed were an answer to prayer, the voice should come from the golden altar itself since the incense is burned on the altar and not on the four horns. In the Old Testament period only the blood of the sin-offering is put on the horns of the golden altar round about (Lev. 16.18). Hence the voice which comes out of the four horns of the golden altar signifies instead that God is going to judge men according to the work of the Lord Jesus. God judges men because they will not accept the gospel and refuse to believe. This is the voice of God because He is the only one behind the golden altar.

9.14 "The great river Euphrates"—This river shall be the boundary in the future (see the prophecies of Ezekiel).

At the sounding of the fifth trumpet Antichrist appears, and at the sounding of the sixth trumpet war breaks out. Antichrist attempts to establish his kingdom.

Whereas the sixth trumpet in chapter 9 tells us of the victory of Antichrist, the sixth bowl in chapter 16 tells us of his defeat.

9.15 These four messengers of the great river Euphrates are slayers. As soon as they are released they commence to kill. God has not ordered them to kill, He only releases them. But they go out to kill, since they are killers by nature. Every prophetic event has its preparation before execution: "the hour and day and month and year"—not only the year and month and day but even the hour are pre-arranged.

The slaying of the fourth part of men in the first four seals refers to all who have been slain during these 20 centuries. The destruction of one third in the first four trumpets is restricted to the earth, the sea, the rivers, and the sky. But the plague in the sixth trumpet affects men directly, and within a short period one third of all mankind on earth will be killed.

9.16 The number of the armies of the horsemen is 200 million. Horses are trained for battle; they are not afraid of guns and cannon.

9.17 Both the horses and the horsemen have breastplates of three colors: fire, purple, and yellow. These breastplates are for self-protection, not for attack. Because the horsemen are human beings they evidently must be specially possessed by demons.

Fire burns, smoke suffocates, and brimstone (sulfur) stinks. All three belong to the lake of fire (cf. 19.3, 21.8).

9.18 The killing is not done by the horsemen but by the horses. Out of the mouths of the horses come forth fire and smoke and brimstone which will destroy one third of all men on earth. Hence it is the mouths of the horses which kill.

9.19 The tails of these horses are like serpents with which they hurt men.

What is given in Deuteronomy 28.49–57 seems to fill out what is not described here in the sixth trumpet.

9.20–21 God permits these plagues to come upon

men that they may repent. But what about the men themselves? They do not repent of the works of their hands but instead commit six special sins. Of these six sins, worshiping demons and idols are sins against God, while murders, sorceries, fornication, and thefts are those against men.

The sixth seal shows men's fear of God's wrath; the sixth trumpet reveals the wickedness of men. After the sixth seal there is given an interpretation of events; and hence, after the sixth trumpet there is an appropriate insertion (see below).

Two sins especially abominable to God are: (1) worshiping idols, and (2) worshiping demons. And why? Because worshiping idols is worshiping that which men have made, while worshiping demons is worshiping what God has created but has fallen.

Three things an idol cannot do: it can neither see, nor hear, nor walk. But this verse does not mention that an idol cannot speak, since the idol mentioned in 13.15 *is* able to speak.

The source of all sins is not recognizing God. Romans 1.24–32 is the explanation of what is happening here.

The Vision Inserted between the Sixth Trumpet and the Seventh Trumpet

10.1-7 "ANOTHER STRONG ANGEL"

10.1 This strong angel points to the Lord for the following reasons.

(1) The Lord manifests himself here as an angel to show that the position He now takes is a return to the Old Covenant.

(2) Here it is a being "arrayed with a cloud", not a

"coming on the clouds" (Matt. 24.30). Since the Lord is enveloped in cloud, this indicates that it is still the time of mystery, for He has yet to manifest His glory.

(3) In chapter 4 it reads that "there was a rainbow round about the throne" (v.3). Here in 10.1 it indicates that "the rainbow was upon his head", so it too is enveloped in the cloud. Although the rainbow signifies the remembrance of grace and mercy by the Lord, such remembrance remains a mystery which yet awaits manifestation.

(4) "And his face was as the sun"—This represents His glory, though at this moment it is still hidden in the cloud.

(5) "And his feet as pillars of fire"—Pillar speaks of stability (see Gal. 2.9; Jer. 1.18), and fire suggests the holiness and righteousness of God (see Ex. 19.16; Heb. 12.29).

10.2 "And he set his right foot upon the sea, and his left upon the earth"—Placing His feet as pillars of fire upon the sea and the earth indicates He is to judge them with the holiness and righteousness of God. "Set" denotes "occupy": wherever His feet are to tread, the same is occupied by Him (Deut. 11.24; Ps. 8.6).

"A little book"—Some say this little book is the Old Testament, others think it refers to Revelation chapters 11–22. However, none of these seems to be satisfactory. There are many evidences pointing towards it being the book mentioned in chapter 5.

(1) In 5.3 and 7 the book is said to be in the hand of the Lamb, but it is still sealed. In 10.2 it is said to be in the hand of the Angel and it is open.

(2) Since in 5.1–3 the book is sealed, nothing is mentioned of its size. Now in 10.2 we find it is opened, it thus being possible to tell of its littleness.

(3) John's eating this little book, as mentioned in

10.9–10, simply indicates that God has revealed these things to him.

(4) "In the days of the voice of the seventh angel" (10.7). As the seventh trumpet sounds, the mystery of God is finished since it has now been manifested. At the opening of the seventh seal the book is still unopened because the seventh seal includes the seven trumpets. The book is opened only after the sounding of the seventh trumpet, for only then is the mystery fulfilled.

(5) In the vision John sees the opened book (10.2,7,8). This does not imply that the book is opened at the sixth trumpet.

(6) 10.11 says "prophesy again", thus showing that the prophecy is divided into two parts. The first part is from the first seal to the blowing of the seventh trumpet; and the second part is from the seventh trumpet to the new heaven and the new earth. After the sounding of the seventh trumpet there come forth the plagues of the seven bowls. How do we know that the second part of the little book not only speaks of the kingdom and the new heaven and new earth but also includes the seven bowls? It is because in 10.10 it is stated that after John has eaten the little book his belly is made bitter though it is sweet as honey in his mouth. And hence there is both bitterness and sweetness, thus proving both blessing and woe are included here.

Since the book is opened at the sounding of the seventh trumpet, it additionally can be said that the first part of the little book is sealed while its second part is open. Consequently, with regard to the prophecy contained in this book, the first part is a mystery; that is to say, it remains a mystery from the first seal to the seventh trumpet—from 6.1 to 11.19. But it can be said that the second part of the prophecy is open since not only in 10.7 is it clearly stated that at the sounding of the seventh trumpet the mystery of

God is finished, but also in 11.15 it is distinctly declared that at that time the kingdom is come. The second part commences with the seventh trumpet (yet not its sounding) and continues on to the new heaven and the new earth, that is, from the time of 12.1 to 22.22.

The judgments of the seven seals and of the seven trumpets constitute the procedure for opening the book with a view to bringing in the kingdom and also eternity.

10.3 "The seven thunders"—The use of the definite article "the" presupposes a familiarity with these thunders. Their voices are frequently heard in this book of Revelation, they being the outbursts of the wrath of God.

"As a lion roareth"—This demonstrates that God being King over all the world, His voice of judgment makes all who hear it tremble with fear.

10.4 The voices of the seven thunders are not to be recorded. Evidently as John is watching the visions he is also writing them down. What God does not wish people to know He forbids to be written. But here, what God allows John to write are what He desires us to know and to understand.

10.5,6 "Things" here include both the dead and the living. "Sware" shows again a return to the Old Covenant position, since in the era of the New Covenant swearing is forbidden.

10.7 As the seventh trumpet is sounded, the mystery of God is finished.

10.8-11 GOD COMMANDS JOHN TO EAT THE LITTLE BOOK

This is an intimation of how anxious God is to tell us of the facts which are to follow. This is in perfect agreement with Revelation 1.1,2.

"Bitter" is bitter (Ruth 1.20) and "sweet" is pleasant (Ps. 119.103).

11.1-2 "TEMPLE . . . ALTAR"

11.1 What is meant by "measure"? (cf. Num. 35.2,5; Ez. 45.1-3; 42.15,20; 48.8,12,15) Measure means protection or a setting apart for God.

"A reed like unto a rod"—What is its significance? Revelation 21.15-17 mentions only a measuring with a reed, without specifying any using of the reed as a rod. This is due to the simple fact that at the time of the new heaven and new earth, sin, Satan, Antichrist, and the false prophet have all been cast into the lake of fire; all is therefore peaceful. The measuring in Revelation 11.1, however, implies a sense of judgment (cf. Prov. 10.13; Ps. 89.32). Whatever is measured is holy and thus protected by God; but what is left unmeasured is dangerous and worldly.

"The temple of God"—Is this temple in heaven or on earth? It is the temple in heaven, for two reasons: (1) it is the only temple emphasized in this book (11.19, 16.17); and (2) the future temple on earth will be desecrated by idols: how, then, can God protect it as though it were holy?

"Altar"—This is not the brazen altar, since the latter stands in the court and is left unmeasured. But the altar mentioned here is measured, and hence must be in the temple itself. Only the altar of incense is in the temple. This is further confirmed by the phrase "them that worship therein" at the end of the verse.

To measure those who worship in the temple is to say that God protects those who are raptured.

11.2 "The court which is without the temple" has reference to the temple on earth. The temple in heaven is the true temple; the temple on earth is considered here to be the court which is without the temple. Although during the time of the Old Testament kings the altars had been erected on high places to worship God, the task of those few kings who were raised up for the purpose of reformation had always been to try to get rid of these altars at the high places. What men had erected was rejected by God. Only during the transitory period of the calling of the nations to Christ did the Jews who became Christians go also to the temple to worship God (Acts. 2.46, 3.1, 5.20).

In the Old Testament period there was a central temple, but in New Testament times there is no physical building called a "church"; for under the New Covenant we are to worship God in spirit and in truth (John 4.23,24). Further, we are called to worship God in the heavenly sanctuary (Heb. 10.19–22).

How does God abolish the earthly temple so as to draw men to worship Him in the heavenly one? The Lord Jesus offered himself as a sacrifice. At His death all the sacrifices were terminated. And seventy years after the birth of Christ the Romans destroyed the temple at Jerusalem. With the result that there is no longer any temple on earth.

Yet here in the passage before us we find the temple on earth again. This, therefore, is a return to the Old Covenant. "The abomination of desolation" mentioned in Matthew 24.15 has reference to an idol, whereas the phrase "the holy place" is a reference to the temple. During the Great Tribulation an idol will be placed in the sanctuary (2 Thess. 2.2–4; Rev. 13.14).

"The holy city" is Jerusalem (Matt. 4.5). Those who worship in the temple above are the people described in 7.9–17.

"Tread under foot" is the same as is spoken of in Luke 21.24. The nations will have domination for 42 months over the holy city.

11.3–12 "TWO WITNESSES"

Who are these two witnesses? Some interpret them as Christian nations, some as certain sects, and some as the gospel preached by Christians. All these interpretations are unsatisfactory because (1) since these two witnesses wear sackcloth, they can have no reference to a group or groups; (2) the miracles they perform as recorded in 11.5–6 are self-defensive and result in killing, and are therefore unlike the miracles performed during the gospel age which are saving in nature; and (3) the dead bodies mentioned in 11.9 cannot point to any group and they certainly cannot typify the gospel.

These two witnesses are two personal witnesses, since (1) witnessing is done by man (Acts 1.8), (2) they are clothed in sackcloth, (3) they are slain, (4) they have their dead bodies, and (5) they are prophets.

Who are they? Some interpreters say they are none other than Elijah and Moses. They maintain that what is mentioned in 11.6 about the power to shut the heaven from raining is an allusion to something that had actually been done by Elijah; and that the power to turn waters into blood is an allusion to what had been done by Moses. But such an interpretation is based only on what the two men do. According to Hebrews 9, "it is appointed unto men once to die, and after this cometh judgment" (v.27). Moses was dead once, how then could he die again? Moses should therefore not be included.

11.3 "My two witnesses"—The way it is presented here seems to imply that everyone who reads this passage should know who these two men are. The words in 11.4 are quoted from Zechariah 4.2,3. "Standing" signifies living. When a person is tired, he sits down; when sick, he lies down; and when dead, he falls down. But these two men are standing. In the entire Bible only two men are recorded as not having died; they are Enoch and Elijah. These two men alone stand before the Lord. (And incidentally, it is said in the apocryphal writings of John that Enoch and Elijah will come.)

"Two witnesses"—This is the number prescribed in the Scriptures for witnessing (cf. Deut. 17.6, 19.15; Matt. 18.16).

"Sackcloth" conveys the thought of bitterness. The New Testament does not command us to wear sackcloth, but in the Old Testament there was such a command (Is. 22.12; Joel 1.13).

What they preached is judgment, not glad tidings. Enoch preached judgment once before (Jude 14–15), and Elijah was a prophet who killed (see 1 Kings 18.40 and 2 Kings 1.10,12). They will yet preach the woeful news, not the glad tidings.

They shall prophesy during the three and a half years of the Great Tribulation.

11.4 "Olive trees" give oil. "Candlesticks" uplift light. Here then are oil and light. These two witnesses stood at the time of the prophet Zechariah (Zech. 4.11–14), they were standing at the time of John's writing the book of Revelation, and they are still standing in our own day.

These two witnesses are "the sons of oil" (Zech. 4.14 Darby), for they are filled with the Holy Spirit.

"The Lord of the earth"—The Jews had their kingdom. God is the Lord of the heaven and the earth (Gen. 11.22). After the destruction of the Jewish nation God was always addressed as the God of heaven (Dan. 2.18,37,44). Now He is again called the Lord of the earth, for God has returned to the position of the Old Covenant period and has once more recognized the Jews as a nation.

What kind of persons are these two men? Perhaps they are the ones who sell oil to the five foolish virgins (Matt. 25.1-2, 8-10a), or possibly they are those who render a little help to those who will be persecuted during the Great Tribulation (Dan. 11.34).

11.5 These two men oppose the whole wide world, including Antichrist. "And if any man shall desire to hurt them . . . must he be killed", thus showing that these two men know even the evil thoughts of the heart. They testify with force, thereby proving they are not preaching the gospel. They perform miracles in order to protect themselves and help the Jews and the remaining Christians during the period of the Great Tribulation. They do not aim at saving souls.

11.6 "Rain" expresses the grace of God. For God "sendeth rain on the just and the unjust" (Matt. 5.45). A not raining suggests that God has withdrawn His grace.

11.7 "The beast that cometh up out of the abyss"— This points to Antichrist. The wild beast is mentioned 36 times in this book of Revelation. Thirty-six is six times six, the number of man. The very name of "wild beast" reveals his nature and work. (The Lamb is mentioned 28 times in this book. Twenty-eight is seven times four. This name expresses the Lord's nature and work as well as denotes His perfect relationships with God and men.)

This beast comes out of the abyss. In 13.1 it is noted that the beast comes up out of the sea, thus confirming that the abyss is beneath the sea.

The abyss is where the devils live. To come out of the abyss presupposes a resuscitation. According to 17.8 we know that this beast has died and is to be resuscitated.

The two witnesses have powers to kill as they wish, but they cannot kill the beast since the latter is a resuscitated beast.

11.8 "The great city"—Human eyes see it as Jerusalem; but according to its significance "spiritually" it "is called Sodom" (a city noted for its crimes) "and Egypt" (that which opposes God). Yet historically it remains as the place where the Lord was crucified.

The manner of death of these two witnesses is perhaps similar to the Lord's crucifixion, because in the original it says: "where *also* their Lord was crucified"—the word "also" seems to emphasize the thought that they die in the same way as their Lord once died. This coincides with the words in Matthew 23.34–35 that some prophets will be killed and crucified.

11.9 "And from among the peoples"—Representatives come from all peoples and nations to view the scene, for they all deem these two men to be public enemies. When they hear that these two men are killed, they come to see it for themselves. In accordance with Joel 3.1–2 and Zechariah 12.3 and 14.2 peoples from all over the earth will gather at Jerusalem.

"Three days and a half"—This number stands between

three days and four days. They are neither incorruptible (just as was the Lord, in His three days of burial—John 2.19; Acts 2.30–31) nor decayed (as was Lazarus, being four days in the grave—John 11.39). And it is John alone who records the three days, the four days, and now these three days and a half.

11.10 As the news spreads over the world, there are celebrations everywhere. "Send(ing) gifts" represents their highest delight. Why are the peoples so happy? Probably because (1) they have suffered physically and (2) their consciences have pricked them greatly.

11.11 "The breath of life"—Resurrection is the work of the Holy Spirit. The phrase "they stood upon their feet" shows that they are alive (whereas in 11.8 dead bodies are said to lie on the ground).

"Great fear fell upon them that beheld them"—These are afraid (1) because of the immediate reason that these two men are suddenly come back to life, and (2) because of the remote reason of what these two men will do after their resurrection since they had such powers before.

11.12 "They went up into heaven in the cloud"— The word "cloud" here is just as definite as the cloud mentioned in 10.1, since both have the definite article before them. When our Lord ascended He was only seen by His disciples. When these two witnesses ascend they will be seen by their enemies so that the latter may know that God alone is the Lord.

11.13,14 "A GREAT EARTHQUAKE"

The city is the city of Jerusalem. The 7,000 persons are persons of renown.

The whole book of Revelation records four earthquakes: at the time of the sixth seal (6.13), in 8.5, in 11.13, and in 11.19 (what is said in 16.18 is the same as in 11.19, for both have the same order of lightnings, and voices, and thunders, and earthquake).

The word "affrighted" and joined together with the subsequent phrase "and give glory to the God of heaven" is not to be construed as meaning they repented. It simply shows that they finally acknowledge that this is God's doing. In 16.11 it clearly states that they refuse to repent (cf. Ex. 8.18,19; 1 Sam. 6.5,6; Joshua 7.19).

[Here ends the vision inserted between the sixth and seventh trumpets.]

11.15–18 THE SEVENTH TRUMPET

This section itemizes the effects of the sounding of the seventh trumpet. The plagues of the seven bowls are the plagues of the seventh trumpet, and these constitute "the third Woe" announced in 11.14.

After 11.16 the thrones on which the 24 elders sit are no longer mentioned, for the kingdom has come. And after 19.4 these elders themselves are seen no more because they have resigned their position of governing the universe.

11.18 "Thy wrath"—The wrath of God is expressed in the plagues of the seven bowls.

Only three classes of people will receive reward: (1) "Thy servants the prophets" (there are also prophets in the New Testament, even those who are spiritually gifted); (2) "the saints", and (3) "them that fear thy name" (there were God-fearing men in the Old Testament; but this designation is not applicable to the New Testament age; so probably these will be the nations that will inherit the kingdom—see Matthew 25.31–46).

The phrase "them that destroy the earth" perhaps includes: (1) those who form Babylon, (2) those who worship and follow the wild beast (13.14), and (3) those mentioned in 20.7–9.

11.19 SITUATION IN HEAVEN AFTER SEVENTH TRUMPET

This verse runs parallel in time with 16.17–21, for both passages show us the situation at the end of the third woe.

PART SIX

THE TRINITY OF SATAN

The Trinity of Satan
(12.1–13.18)

A sign appears to tell people what is to be expected.

Beginning in 12.1 the apostle John again prophesies, in accordance with the words of chapter 10—"Thou must prophesy again" (v.11).

Hence the portion of Revelation from 12.1 to 22.21 is a prophesying again, with a view to supplementing the first part which runs from chapter 6 to chapter 11. The first part (6–11) gives the outline in order, while the second part (12–22) presents the details.

In 11.15 the great voices in heaven are recorded as saying: "The kingdom of the world is become the kingdom of our Lord, and of his Christ: and he shall reign for ever and ever"—This word projects itself beyond to the new heaven and the new earth, for this kingdom is to go on forever and ever. Thus chapters 6–11 may be considered as speaking on to the point of the new heaven and the new earth. Chapters 12–22 take up the vital points belonging to the first part by explaining them in detail. Just as Genesis 1 speaks of what God has done in the six days, Genesis 2 treats specifically of what God does on the sixth day. In this matter of treatment, therefore, Revelation 6–11 can be compared to Genesis 1, and Revelation 12–22 to Genesis 2.

The star fallen from heaven to the earth in 9.1 is the same person as the great red dragon spoken of in 12.3.

Chapters 12–14 are written symbolically, while matters mentioned in chapters 15–16 are presented literally, with the contents of chapters 17 and 18 again being shown in symbolic fashion. For it should be noted that the wrath of God and His judgment are never presented symbolically; they are always given in literal form.

12.1 Some suggest that this woman is Mary, but such an interpretation is incorrect because (1) it is inconceivable that Mary could possess the glory depicted in 12.1; (2) this woman already has other children (12.17), but the Lord Jesus is the firstborn of Mary; and (3) this kind of interpretation is contrary to the very nature of this prophetic book. If the woman is Mary and the man child is Christ, then this would be historical and not prophetic in nature. Yet this book is the very revelation of Jesus Christ.

Who, then, is the woman? Before answering directly, let us make the following observations:

(1) All single women mentioned in this book point to some city (17.18; 21.9,10).

(2) J. K. Seiss has indicated that the sun represents the Lord, the moon the power of darkness, and the twelve stars the twelve tribes of Israel. It is within reason to say that the sun speaks of Christ and the twelve stars the twelve tribes (Israel), but what is the basis for saying that the moon stands for the power of darkness? Robert Govett has stated that the sun suggests grace which idea is acceptable, that the moon represents the law which thought is totally unacceptable, and that the stars stand for the twelve tribes of Israel which interpretation is also acceptable. The difficulty lies in explaining the moon.

Thus there are those who claim that these sun, moon, and stars all point to Christians. Their basis for so interpreting is in 1 Corinthians 15.41. Yet there is a great

difference between the stars mentioned in 1 Corinthians
15.41 and the stars here in 12.1. For the stars in the latter
case are described as "*twelve* stars"—a specific rather than
general reference.

Our answer is: this woman signifies Jerusalem of the
nation of Israel. And the reasons are as follows.

(1) By reading Genesis 37.9–10 we readily know that
the sun stands for Jacob, the moon for his wife, and the
twelve stars for the twelve tribes of Israel. Since the sun,
moon, and stars are spoken of together, this leads us to
believe that the woman is the city of Jerusalem—which
represents the nation of Israel.

(2) "*Arrayed with* the sun", not the sun itself, is what is in
view here. This distinguishes her as the mother of Israel.
The phrase "and the moon under her feet" is to indicate
how she is being forgotten, while the words "and upon her
head a crown of twelve stars" clearly stand for the twelve
tribes of Israel.

(3) "Travailing in birth" (12.2). In Isaiah 26.17–18, in
Jeremiah 6.22–25 (where Zion is Jerusalem), 13.19–21 and
30.6–7, and in Micah 4.8–10 and 5.1–3, all these prophets
announce beforehand that Jerusalem will be in pangs as a
woman is found in travail.

(4) The archangel Michael comes to help. According to
Daniel 12.1, at the time of trouble Michael shall stand up
for the children of Israel.

(5) God orders the woman to flee to the wilderness
(12.6,14). According to Matthew 24.16–21 our Lord clearly
tells them to flee (cf. also Luke 21.20–24).

Why are Christians considered as coming out of Jerusalem? Because (1) the Lord is the Lion of the tribe of Judah
(Rev. 5.5), (2) salvation is from the Jews (John 4.22), and
(3) the Jerusalem above is our mother (Gal. 4.26).

[*Translator's Note:* In the author's book which in Chinese is entitled *Holy and Without Blemish* (first published at Shanghai in 1953, with a later Chinese edition published at Hong Kong under the title *The Glorious Church*), Mr. Nee came to a more matured understanding concerning the significance of "the woman" in Revelation 12. There he posed the same question: Who is this woman? In the following paragraphs, translated directly from pages 78 and 79 of the Shanghai, 1953 edition, the reader will find the author's answer.]

In the Old Testament record there is only one woman who had an encounter with the serpent, and she is Eve of Genesis 3. Now in the New Testament there is also one woman who had a skirmish with the serpent, and she is this woman of Revelation 12. This shows the unity of the Bible. Here God purposely mentions that the great dragon is the old serpent, thus distinguishing it as the one, same and only old serpent. Likewise, this woman will also be the same woman as in the Garden. Moreover, as there are sun, moon and stars mentioned in Genesis 1, so there are sun, moon and stars spoken of here. As there is the serpent in Genesis 3, so the serpent is present here. As the seed of the woman is mentioned in Genesis 3, so the seed of the woman is also shown here. And as travail in birth is predicted in Genesis 3, so travail in birth is presented here. By studying these two passages of the Scriptures together we may conclude that this woman is none other than the woman who has been foreordained in the eternal purpose of God and who will experience such things as these at the last days. Hence we may say that the woman mentioned in Genesis 2 reveals the eternal will of God; the woman seen in Ephesians 5 unveils the position and future of the church; the woman spoken of in Revelation 12 discloses that which will happen at the last days; and there is yet a woman who will declare what is going to be in eternity.

When this woman appears in the vision now before us, the Bible describes her as "arrayed with the sun, and the moon under her feet, and upon her head a crown of twelve stars"—And these descriptions have their dispensational meanings:

(1) This woman is arrayed with the sun—the sun points to the Lord Jesus. Since the woman is arrayed with the sun, this indicates that the sun shines at its brightest hour upon the woman. In this dispensation God is manifesting himself through her. This is her relationship with Christ and with the dispensation of grace.

(2) This woman has the moon under her feet—the word "under" does not imply "tread upon"; in the Greek the word simply means a lying under her feet. The light of the moon is not self-producing but is reflective. Things in the dispensation of law only reflect the things in the dispensation of grace, for the law is but a shadow. The holy temple, the ark, the incense and the shewbread, the sacrifices which the priests offer, and even the blood of the bullocks and lambs—all these are types. The moon being under the woman's feet shows how the things of the law are subjected to her, that is to say, they belong to her. So that this description tells of the woman's relationship with the dispensation of law.

(3) This woman wears upon her head a crown of twelve stars—the distinguished personages who figured during the dispensation of the patriarchs may be counted from Abraham up to the birth of the twelve tribes of Israel. Wearing such a crown of twelve stars shows the relationship between this woman and the dispensation of the patriarchs.

From the above observations we can understand that this woman is related not only to the dispensation of grace but also to the dispensations of law and of the patriarchs, although here her relationship with the dispensation of grace is most intimate. And hence representationally this woman includes in herself the people found in the dispensations of the patriarchs and of law as well as in the dispensation of grace.

[Here ends the translated portion taken directly from Mr. Nee's *Holy and Without Blemish* (Shanghai, 1953), pp. 78–79.—*Translator*]

12.3 "A great red dragon"—He is the same as "the old serpent" or "the Devil" or "Satan" found in 12.9. This serpent is the very one spoken of in Genesis 3.1. "Red" is the color of war. As a great red dragon he is a killer from the beginning to the end (cf. John 8.44; 1 John 5.19).

"Seven heads" (see 17.9,12)—Ten horns represent the kings under the great king. The head is bigger than the horn and it is the head that makes use of the horns. Hence the dragon will use the so-called revived Roman Empire together with these lesser kings to persecute God's children.

12.4 "The third part of the stars of heaven, . . . cast them to the earth"—These stars are the angels cited in 12.9. The third part of the angels of heaven has followed the devil. The casting down of the dragon will occur after the man child is raptured.

12.5 Who is this "man child"? Some say it represents the children of Israel, but this is not possible due to the following reasons:

(1) The sun, moon and stars already represent the nation of Israel.

(2) This man child is caught up to the throne. The Bible never suggests that the nation of Israel will be raptured, for

such a thought is in direct conflict with the prophecies concerning the nation of Israel.

(3) This man child trusts in the blood of the Lamb (12.11), but the nation of Israel does not. Some people have even advanced the theory that at the time of the Great Tribulation many of the children of Israel will believe in the Lord. Yet the Bible has not said this. What the Scriptures do say is that when the feet of the Lord Jesus shall touch the Mount of Olives God will open a fountain of salvation for the children of Israel, and then and there they will be saved (Zech. 13.1, 14.4, 12.10–14).

Some others advocate the interpretation of Christ being the man child, but this is also inapplicable for the following reasons:

(1) The woman represents Jerusalem, while the Lord Jesus is born in Bethlehem.

(2) This man child is not personal but corporate in character (12.10–11).

(3) Should this man child be Christ, the dragon will then be Herod, yet 12.9 states explicitly that the dragon is Satan himself.

(4) As soon as the man child is born, he is caught up to the throne, whereas the Lord Jesus is taken up to heaven only after He has lived over thirty years, died, and been raised from the dead.

(5) Because all this is a vision, the word "travail" cannot be interpreted literally.

Still others say that the man child denotes the whole church. This too is impossible since (1) the whole church is not all raptured at the same time: some will go in advance of others and some will follow afterwards, but here the man child is caught up as a unit simultaneously; (2) to rule all the nations with an iron rod is not a promise given to the entire church, rather is it promised to the overcomers only (2.26–27), and not all in the church are overcomers; and (3) to reign is promised to those who suffer and endure with the Lord today (2 Tim. 2.12).

Who, then, is this man child? He must be the overcomers: for example, (1) some Christians in the church in Smyrna, since "Be thou faithful unto death" (2.10) coincides with the last clause in 12.11—"they loved not their life even unto death"; (2) some Christians in the church in Thyatira, for "he shall rule them with a rod of iron" (2.26,27) agrees with "a man child, who is to rule all the nations with a rod of iron" (12.5); (3) some Christians in the church in Philadelphia, because they are kept out of "the hour of trial" (3.10) just as the man child is "caught up unto God" (12.5); and (4) some Christians in the church in Laodicea, since they will "sit" on the "throne" (3.21) just as the man child "is to rule all the nations" (12.5).

Accordingly, those represented by the man child are not the whole church but are the overcomers within the church.

In our discussion of chapter 7 we have already listed eight points of similarity between the great multitude spoken of there and the man child mentioned here. For the man child represents a portion of that countless number. (Please note that chapter 7 deals with the general topic of rapture, whereas chapter 12 gives the details of some part of those raptured.)

[*Translator's Note:* In his later work, already quoted from above, Mr. Nee in *Holy and Without Blemish* elaborates on the meaning of the man child. The following four paragraphs are translated directly from pages 81–84 of the Shanghai, 1953 edition.]

Verse 5 "And she was delivered of a son, a man child,

who is to rule all the nations with a rod of iron: and her child was caught up unto God, and unto his throne"—In order to know the relationship between this man child and the woman, please read Galatians—"But the Jerusalem that is above is free, which is our mother" (4.26). Read also the last clause in the next verse: "For more are the children of the desolate than of her that hath the husband" (v.27). The Jerusalem above is the New Jerusalem, which is the woman whom God has prepared to have in eternity to come. She is none other than Eve in creation, the body of Christ in the dispensation of grace, this woman whom we see at the close of the dispensation of grace, and the New Jerusalem God will have in the eternity to come. A having many children does not suggest that the mother is separated from the children; rather does it mean that the one is divided into many, yet the many are combined into one. By adding up these many children you have the mother. It is not a case of a mother with five children making six, but a case of the five children making up the one mother. Each child is a part of the mother, who imparts a little of herself to each child. They seem as though they are begotten of her, yet actually they are but her own self. Thus the mother is not one who stands alongside her children but is the sum total of many children that are in view. This is a very special principle.

In chapter 12 the man child whom the woman delivers is subject to the same principle. This being a vision, it is symbolic in character. The word "delivered" here does not imply the idea of the child coming out and being separated from the woman, it instead implies that within the woman there is such a man child. In other words, a class of people is included in this woman. All the people of God are ordained to have a share in the eternal purpose and plan of God. Due to their failure in taking up responsibility, however, God chooses from among them a number of people. The people whom God has chosen from the many form the man child. The mother represents the whole, the man child represents the remnant. This man child is the "brethren" mentioned in verse 10. He is not one person but is a considerable number of people—a composite of many; though in comparison with the mother, this man child is only a minority. Nevertheless, in spite of their smallness in number as compared to the whole body, the plan and purpose of God is upon them.

"And she was delivered of a son, a man child, who is to rule all the nations with a rod of iron" (v.5). Three times in the book of Revelation is this ruling with an iron rod mentioned. The first time is in 2.26,27: "And he that overcometh, and he that keepeth my works unto the end, to him will I give authority over the nations: and he shall rule them with a rod of iron"—This most distinctly points to the overcomers in the church. The last time is in 19.15: "And out of his mouth proceedeth a sharp sword, that with it he should smite the nations: and he shall rule them with a rod of iron"—This is in reference to the Lord Jesus.

Now then, to whom does this verse in 12.5 refer? If it is not applicable to the overcomers in the church it must have reference to the Lord Jesus. Yet can it mean the Lord Jesus here? It is highly improbable (though not absolutely impossible, since later on we will observe that the Lord Jesus is also included). Why is it not probable? Because as soon as the man child is born he is caught up to the throne of God. It thus indicates that the man child cannot be Christ since the Lord Jesus when on the earth lived for over 33 years, died, and was raised from the dead before He ascended. Hence we believe this man child signifies the overcomers in the church. He represents a part of the church, that part which overcomes. Nonetheless, the man child also *includes* the Lord Jesus since He is the first overcomer and all other overcomers are included in Him.

[Here ends the translated portion taken directly from Mr. Nee's *Holy and Without Blemish* (Shanghai, 1953), pp. 81–84.—*Translator*]

12.6 "And the woman fled"—This is the same flight as is depicted in Matthew 24.6–20 and Luke 21.20–24. In 12.1 the woman is seen in heaven, but now in 12.6 she is in the wilderness. After the man child is born she loses her heavenly position. She is now none else but the Jerusalem on earth. A wilderness is a place both barren and uninhabited. God nourishes her as He did the children of Israel in the days of the Exodus.

In Galatians 4.21–31 we have a contrast: one is the heavenly Jerusalem, the other is the earthly Jerusalem; one represents the Christians, the other, the Jews; one is typified by Israel, the other, by Ishmael. The essential thought in all this is to prove that we Christians are free in the same way as Isaac was free.

12.7–9 "WAR IN HEAVEN"

12.7 War is inevitable. Who is to dwell in heaven—the man child or the dragon? The man child is to occupy the dragon's territory, therefore there is war.

In the whole Bible, only one archangel is named—Michael, whose name means "Who is like God?" (some interpreters even think that Michael is the Lord Jesus).

During the days of Job the dragon could appear before the presence of God. At the time of Christ he still could appear. But at the time of the rapture of the man child, he no longer can.

12.8,9 The name dragon speaks of cruelty; old serpent, of deceit; devil, of seduction; and Satan, of opposition. The devil is cast down from heaven, along with a third part of the angels who follow him, and he opens the pit of the abyss (9.1). How very dark is this world!

12.10–12 "A GREAT VOICE"

12.10 Formerly God redeemed with the blood, but now He redeems with power. The authority of the kingdom of God is perfect at the throne; but before Satan is cast down, God's will is not done in the air. After 1260 days the kingdom of God will come upon the earth, and then shall His will be done on earth also. (The casting out of demons recorded in Matthew 12.28 is a proof that the kingdom of God has come upon the earth.)

12.11 Three things are essential for overcoming the accuser: (1) The blood. (Since the accusations may not always be false, the blood is imperative for us.) We rest in the precious blood of the Lamb (Rom. 8.31–34). (2) The word of the testimony. Not only what the heart believes, but also what the mouth confesses concerning the same heart belief. As the word is spoken, Satan becomes helpless. (3) An attitude of not fearing death. The greatest of all temptations is death. If we maintain a right attitude, Satan is beaten.

12.12 In Revelation 13.1 a beast is mentioned as coming up out of the sea (Antichrist). In 13.11 it is recorded that a beast (the false prophet) comes up out of the earth. In 9.1 the Bible says that "a star" (the dragon) is fallen from heaven. When these three come upon the earth, there is "woe for the earth and the sea" as is stated here in verse 12.

The premonition of Satan ("knowing that he hath but a short time") is comparable to the deduction that an historian might arrive at.

During the tribulation there is the wrath of God as well as the wrath of Satan.

12.13-17 "THE DRAGON . . . PERSECUTED THE WOMAN"

12.13 Many Old Testament prophets had made predictions concerning these events mentioned here and in the succeeding verses. During the time of the Great Tribulation the city of Jerusalem will be under the siege of nations. In persecuting the woman, the dragon is but carrying out his "great wrath" mentioned in the preceding verse.

12.14 Since the woman is symbolic, the wings must also be symbolic. God will give her a supernatural power to run fast. When God led the children of Israel out of Egypt He carried them as the eagle does its eaglets on its wings (Ex. 19.4; Deut. 32.11,12). The Jews at that time will receive special protection from God.

12.15 Since the "serpent" is Satan, the "water" mentioned here must mean something else too. By reading Jeremiah 46.7,8 we know that water signifies the rushing of enemy armies (cf. also Jer. 47.2,4; Is. 59.19). As the dragon casts water after the woman, so Satan will use the armies of the nations to pursue the children of Israel.

12.16 "Earth" is earth. In Exodus 15.10 we see that God uses water to overturn the Egyptian army; in Numbers

16.30 we read that He opens the earth to swallow up the rebellious; and now He uses the earth again in the same way to protect the chosen race.

12.17 The phrase "the rest of her seed" includes the faithful Jews and the Christians who are left behind. If these words refer only to the Jews it cannot be said of them that they "keep the commandments of God, and hold the testimony of Jesus", since at this juncture the Lord has not yet returned to earth nor have the Jews believed in Him.

The word "saints" in 13.7 comprises in its meaning both the Jews and the Christians who are left behind. And hence they are the same people as is "the rest of the [woman's] seed" spoken of in 12.17.

13.1–10 "A BEAST COMING UP OUT OF THE SEA"

The sea points to the Mediterranean, and the beast represents either a kingdom—that of the Roman Empire—or a person who is Antichrist.

If the beast means a kingdom, the sea needs to be interpreted spiritually. If the beast represents a person, the sea must be taken literally. Spiritually interpreted, "sea" stands for the Gentiles since the land is spiritually reckoned as the Jews. This is in accordance with the way the Scriptures explain the sea. "The waters which thou sawest, when the harlot sitteth, are peoples, and multitudes, and nations, and tongues" (17.15). We find in Daniel 7.3,7 that the sea indicates the Gentile world too. And hence a coming up out of the sea means a coming forth from the Gentile world.

"A beast coming up out of the sea"—The Roman Empire will revive. The sea discloses its location and the beast reveals its character.

13.1 "Ten horns" represent ten minor kings (17.12), while "seven heads" speak of seven supreme kings (17.10). Since the heads are bigger than the horns and the latter are on the heads, the seven heads and ten horns must stand for seven emperors and ten kings.

The "seven heads" indicate seven successive emperors, whereas the "ten horns" speak of ten contemporary kings. (Altogether, the ancient Roman Empire had thirteen Caesars, among whom five, at the time of John the Apostle, died violently. The term "fallen" (17.10) in the original bears in it the sense of a violent death. The sixth Caesar, Domitian, it should be recalled, was also slain. And the seventh one will likewise be killed. So that all seven Roman Emperors mentioned by God do not die peacefully. The ten horns are but subordinate kings to Rome.)

Antichrist is the beast as well as the seventh head. 12.3 reads: "Upon his heads seven diadems"; and the next chapter says: "On his horns ten diadems" (13.1). Antichrist in the days to come will arise from the revived Roman Empire so as to gain control over Europe. According to the historical narration the ten kings alluded to in 12.3 are not yet crowned, nor do they have authority. But after these ten kings *are* crowned and receive authority they will crown the beast. And thus Antichrist gains authority at that very time.

"Blasphemy"—Whatever exalts oneself and abases God is blasphemy (see Matt. 9.3, 26.65; John 5.18, 10.33; Mark 3.28; Rev. 16.21).

"Upon his heads names of blasphemy"—It means that these heads call themselves gods. History informs us that the first five Caesars in the Roman Empire demanded the people to worship them as gods.

13.2 "Leopard"—In order to understand this section we must read Daniel 2.31–33 and 7.3–8. By so doing we learn that (1) the lion is the golden head in Nebuchadnez-zar's image, (2) the bear is Medo-Persia—the breast of silver, (3) the leopard has a belly of brass and thus represents Greece, and (4) the fourth beast, terrible and powerful, which was diverse from the other beasts, has the legs of iron—which is the Roman Empire. Babylon is terrible in war, Medo-Persia is slow but savage, Greece is ferocious, and Rome is cruel.

The beast of 13.2 possesses all four bad characters. In fact, it is the composite of all the powers of the nations.

The book of Revelation speaks of the Lord Jesus as the Lamb 28 times, and the beast it speaks of as the wild beast 36 times.

God will make use of the beast to judge the world (Jer. 5.6, Hosea 13.7, Hab. 1.8). The leopard has spots, thus signifying having sins (Jer. 13.23). Both the bear and the lion tore people apart (see 2 Kings 2.24 on how the bears tore up the 42 lads, read Daniel 6.22 on how God sealed the mouths of the lions against Daniel, and read 2 Tim. 4.17 on how God delivered Paul out of the lion's mouth).

The beast we read about in 13.2 points to a kingdom because it has seven heads and ten horns. According to 17.9,10,12 a kingdom is no doubt meant. The lion, the bear and the leopard mentioned in Daniel 7 are all symbolic of kingdoms; and hence the fourth beast must also be a kingdom—that of the Roman Empire.

But the beast of 13.2 likewise refers to a person. The term "fallen" used in 17.8–11 means meeting violent death, and the one who still remained at the time of the Apostle John was Domitian; therefore the beast spoken of in 19.20 and 20.10 is no doubt a man with personality. God does not cast a kingdom into the lake of fire.

13.3,14 "As though it had been smitten unto death" —The image must be that of a man, for Antichrist is a human being. The dragon counterfeits God; the beast, Christ; and the false prophet, the Holy Spirit.

The false father also gives authority to the false son so that the latter may have the power to perform lying wonders (2 Thess. 2.9). The phrase "lying wonders" does not mean to convey the idea that these wonders are false; it simply means that the purpose of these wonders is to deceive people.

"His throne" (13.2)—This indicates that there must be a kingdom. No kingdom, then no throne. The dragon revives the Roman Empire and gives it to the false christ.

Note that 13.3 says this: "as though it had been smitten unto death"; and chapter 13 further comments on it by saying: "the stroke of the sword" (v.14). In connection with 17.7,8, it should be noted that John wrote this book of Revelation in approximately 96 A.D. Hence the word "was" must refer to the time before 96 A.D.; "is not", to the time when John wrote this book; and "is about to come up out of the abyss, and to go into perdition", to the time in the future. According to 17.9–11, "the five are fallen, the one is" (this latter one, at the time of John, was Domitian); "the other is not yet come" (one wonders if he is now already in the world, but only waiting to be manifested). Judging by the words in verse 11, there are seven souls, seven bodies; yet eight live, for the eighth one is also one of the original seven. He must have died and is to be reanimated in the days to come. There will arise a most powerful person who will revive the Roman Empire and become the leader of a confederacy of ten kingdoms. He will be killed, but he will also be reanimated. Thus, the whole world will consider him as god. Actually, he is not resurrected in the real sense;

he is only reanimated by the entering into his body of the soul of one of the former Emperors.*

Many people do not believe in the resurrection of Christ, and yet they all shall believe in the reanimation of Antichrist.

13.4 Antichrist is so influential because the dragon is backing him. People worship the beast because they consider him superior both in personality and power.

13.5 "Speaking great things"—that is, exalting one's own self; "and blasphemies"—defying God. The "authority" given, as mentioned in this verse, is permitted by God and is of a restricted nature. The number "forty and two" is the multiplication of seven and six. Seven is a perfect number, but six is a satanic one. We notice that in Numbers there were 42 stations from the Exodus to Canaan; and in 2 Kings we note that the bears tore up 42 lads: in the Bible the number 42 stands for wandering and judgment. In reading 2 Thessalonians 2.9–11 we learn the reason God allows Satan to go on a rampage for 42 months. The word "lie" in verse 11 has a definite article before it in the original Greek. It should therefore properly be read as "*the* lie", which may refer back to Genesis 3 where we read that Satan lied by saying "shall not surely" and "shall be as God" (vv.4,5).

13.6 The first thing the beast does is to blaspheme God, for the name of God includes all the personality, nature, and authority of God. The phrase "his tabernacle" points to heaven.

---

* *Not* to be construed as teaching reincarnation. See explanatory footnote at 17.11 below.—*Translator*

13.7 "To make war with the saints"—These latter are the Christians who are kept behind and those Jews who are faithful to God. The influence of the beast is world-wide, though his kingdom is limited to the revived Roman Empire.

13.8 This verse proves that there will yet be Christians on earth, for there will still be people whose names are written in the Lamb's book of life. It is by the power of God's election that they are being kept from succumbing to temptation.

13.9 "If any man hath an ear, let him hear"—In the time of chapters 2 and 3 the churches still hold their position as such, hence each time there is added the clause: "what the Spirit saith to the churches"; here, though, only some Christians still remain behind, and therefore the exhortation simply reads: "If any man hath an ear, let him hear."

13.10 Christians cannot rise up, as the Crusaders did, to fight against their enemies. They can only practice patience. If they lose their patience they will lose their faith.

13.11–18 "ANOTHER BEAST COMING UP OUT OF EARTH"

13.11 This beast is also a wild beast. Because he is to come up out of the earth he must also be a re-vitalized person, since Hades is beneath the earth. On the other hand, "earth" may have reference to the Jewish nation. The Scriptures often classify the earth as being symbolic of the nation of Israel.

This beast is the false prophet. He is a person since (1) three times the Bible calls him the false prophet (16.13,

19.20, 20.10), (2) the Lord has clearly stated that there will be false prophets (Matt. 24.24), and (3) there are three evil spirits: Satan, the beast (Antichrist), and another beast (the false prophet). Each has his mission to fulfill. Thus this beast cannot be a system but a person. At the time of evil, we have the counterfeit of the triune God.

"Two horns"—Since this beast is a person and not a kingdom, his two horns should signify two spirits; for the horns of the Lamb are referred to as being the Spirit of God (5.6), and the horns of the beast are like to those of the Lamb. "To give breath to it" (13.15) may be translated "to give spirit to it"; this is one spirit, and 16.13 tells of another spirit.

"And he spake as a dragon"—His speech is both deceitful and atrocious. Just as the first beast sits on the throne of the dragon, so this beast speaks the word of the dragon.

13.12 This second beast works by means of the authority of the first beast. As the Holy Spirit is the executor as well as the power in the Godhead, so the false prophet is the executor and the power of the trio of evil. "To worship" here is compulsory, unlike that mentioned in 13.4 which is voluntary.

There are many evidences to link the first beast with the revitalization of Nero. This second beast may very well be the return from the dead of the betrayer Judas. Acts 1.20, Psalm 69.25 and Psalm 109.8 all point to Judas, for Acts 1.20 quotes from Psalms 69 and 109. Psalm 109.6 declares: "Let Satan stand at his right hand" (mg.)—This is yet to be fulfilled. At the time of Christ, Satan entered into the heart of Judas; but not until the time of Revelation 13.12 will Satan stand at his right hand. We are also told in Acts 1:

"that he might go to his own place" (v.25). Concerning other individuals the Scriptures always say he is "gathered to his own people" or that "he is gone down into sheol"; but in the case of Judas we are told that "he might go to his own place"—as though he has a special place set aside for his use. In the entire New Testament the term "son of perdition" is only used twice: one is found in John 17.12 which distinctly points to Judas, and the other is found in 2 Thessalonians 2.3 which alludes to Antichrist. If the first beast is Antichrist, the son of perdition, who else can be the second beast except Judas who also is called the son of perdition? In John 6 the Lord is recorded as calling Judas "a devil" (v.70). So then, who but Judas can rank among the trio of evil?

13.13 The greatest sign he will perform is that of making fire come down from heaven. This perhaps is for the purpose of counteracting the fire which the two witnesses draw down to the earth.

13.14,15 Here is the consummation of idolatry. Just as the Lord, after His resurrection, bears the marks of wounds which He once showed to Thomas, so the sword wound of the beast remains visible to people so as to convince them of his revitalization.

"Breath" may also be translated "spirit"—after the spirit is given, there will naturally be breath. This beast possesses three characteristics: (1) to give breath, (2) to make the image speak, and (3) to cause those to be killed who do not worship the image of the beast. This is quite different from what is mentioned in Psalm 135.15–17 and Jeremiah 10.3ff. In ancient times the images or idols had mouths but spoke not, had eyes but saw not, had ears but heard not, neither was there any breath found in their mouths. In the future, though, the image of the beast *will* have breath.* How the image of the beast can kill people is not revealed to us. It may be that the image of the beast will announce a sentence of death and people will then be put to death, or it may even possess some kind of mechanism by which to kill people.

13.16 "A mark"—This mark must be visible. Since it is stamped on the human body, it must by physical in nature. When people buy or sell, this mark can easily be distinguished. To be so marked means that the soul and body of the man belong to Satan. He is to be an open, not a secret, follower of Satan. No doubt such people do not have Christ in them.

13.17 It is hard not to sell, but it is harder not to buy. The mark can be of various kinds, with some bearing the name of the beast and others the number of his name.

13.18 Many have attempted to find out what the number 666 is, but they fail to see the unity of this verse. Three things need to be joined in one: *First*, "the number of a man" (the number of a place is therefore discounted). *Second*, "the number of the beast"—In 13.1 it is stated that the beast has seven heads, and in 17.9,10 it is stated that the seven heads are "the seven mountains", also they are "the seven kings" (the city of Rome is alone built on seven hills). Which does the beast represent—the Roman Empire or one of the emperors of Rome? Since 13.18 says that the number of the beast is the number of a man, the beast cannot stand for the Roman Empire but rather points to one of the

---

* But see explanatory footnote on this at 17.11 below.—*Translator*

Roman emperors. *And third*, "the number of [a man's] name", which is also the number of the name of a Roman emperor, must be 666. From the convergence of these three points we may find out who the beast is.

In both Greek and Hebrew, the letters of the alphabet are also used for numbers. Apart from Nero Caesar there is no one else in history who fits this number. The number of Nero is 306, and the number for Caesar is 360. The Bible usually mentions the name of a Roman Emperor together with the title caesar, such as in Luke 2.1 and 3.1 we have Caesar Augustus and Tiberius Caesar. History tells us that Nero always called himself Caesar.

The name Nero Caesar in Hebrew makes up 666, as follows:*

Greek	Hebrew		Greek	Hebrew	
Ne	נ	50	Kai	ק	100
R	ר	200	Sa	ס	60
O	ו	6	R	ר	200
N	נ	50			
	Νερων =	306		Καισαρ =	360 = 666

---

* Robert Govett, *The Apocalypse Expounded*. London: Chas. J. Thynne, 1920, p. 351.—*Translator*

PART SEVEN

THE FIRST FRUITS, THE HARVEST,

AND THE VINTAGE

The First Fruits, the Harvest, and the Vintage
(14.1–20)

14.1 Is Mount Zion in heaven or on earth? It is the heavenly Jerusalem, not the earthly one, because (1) the Mount Zion on earth is at that time in the hands of the Gentiles (11.2); (2) it is clearly stated in 14.4 that "these were purchased from among men", thus implying that they no longer stand on the earthly Mount Zion during that moment; (3) by joining the last two clauses of 14.4 with Exodus 23.19 we learn that the first fruits are not left in the field since as soon as they are ripened they are to be brought to the house of God (see also Ex. 34.26), and since the 144,000 are the first fruits they cannot be left in the field—which speaks of the world (Matt. 13.38)—but are placed instead on the Mount Zion in heaven which is the New Jerusalem; (4) 14.3 says "they sing . . . before the throne, and before the four living creatures and the elders"—thus all these are in heaven and not on the earth; (5) the people referred to in 14.1–5 are the first fruits while those alluded to in 14.14–16 are the harvest, so if the harvesting is unto the air, can the first fruits be gathered elsewhere except to heaven? and (6) there is, moreover, no reason to suggest it as being the Mount Zion on earth since the Lord Jesus will come to the earth only by the time of chapter 19.

Who are the 144,000? The 144,000 cited in Revelation

7.4 and 144,000 spoken of here in 14.1 are two different classes of people, contrasted as follows:

(1) The people of 7.4 are the chosen among the children of Israel, while those of 14.1 are purchased from among men.

(2) The seals received by them are not the same. The one spoken of in 7.2 is "the seal of the living God", which is Old Testament terminology. The seal alluded to in 14.1 bears the name of the Lamb and the name of the Father, and such names are related to the church. Hence these people must come from the church.

(3) The people told about in 7.3 are called "the servants of our God", but those in view in 14.1 are the children of God (this conclusion is deduced from the name of the Father).

(4) Throughout the entire book of Revelation the Lord calls God as Father each time. And He always says it in connection with the church (1.6, 2.27, 3.5, 3.21). The Lord never uses it in connection with Israel.

(5) The people spoken of in 14.1ff. are associated with the Lamb (standing with the Lamb, having the name of the Lamb, following the Lamb, and being the first fruits unto the Lamb). In chapter 7 the Lord is seen as another angel; and this, as we have seen, is a returning to His Old Testament position.

(6) The song they sing is described in 14.3 as a new song, whereas the song the people mentioned in 7.4 sing is but an old song.

(7) The people in view in 14.4 are virgins, but with Israel virginity is to be bewailed. (According to Ex. 23.26, Deut. 7.14, 1 Sam. 2.5, and Ps. 113.9, to bear children is considered a blessing while to be barren is deemed a curse. In Judges 11.38,39 the daughter of Jephthah is said to have bewailed her virginity for two months.)

(8) The articles preceding both of the 144,000 numbers cited in 14.1 and 7.4 are indefinite, and are therefore general and not specific. Thus these 144,000 numbers constitute two different classes.

14.1 The group of 144,000 here is a special class of people in the church; they are not all the people of the church. And the reasons for this conclusion are as follows:

(1) Since the 144,000 figure in 7.4 is taken literally, the number here should also be reckoned as literal.

(2) This group being the first fruits (14.4), it cannot be said that the entire church makes up the first fruits.

(3) There is no such fact that the people in the entire church keep their virginity.

(4) Prior to the arrival of the Great Tribulation (for it is before the voices of the three angels are heard, 14.6–11), these people are already raptured to Mount Zion.

(5) 14.5 tells of the exceptional features of these people, concerning which it cannot be said that all the born-again ones possess such characteristics.

Consequently, the 144,000 standing on Mount Zion are the best of the overcomers of the church; that is to say, this group of 144,000 is representative of the totality of the overcomers.

14.2 "A voice from heaven"—This must be the voice of the 144,000. Their voice is as pleasant as the voice of harps, as awesome as the voice of thunders, and as majestic as the voice of many waters.

14.3 A new song which they alone can sing. All Christians are purchased out of the earth, but these are brought home first.

14.4 Twice we find the words "these are", thus showing that the verse describes and explains who the 144,000 are:

(1) "These are they that were not defiled with women; for they are virgins"—We may not spiritualize the word "women" into "idols", for the Bible does not support such an interpretation. Neither can we consider "women" as representing evil doctrines. Instead, "women" in the Bible is frequently translated "wives"; for example, the Greek word used for "wives" in Acts 21.5 is the same as used for "women" here in 14.4. The Scriptures not only mention this group of 144,000 as being undefiled with women but they also emphasize that they are virgins. This thus indicates that this portion of Scripture is not speaking of purity but of virginity. With this conclusion Matthew 19.10–12 agrees perfectly. Judging by 14.1 here, those whom God has given such a gift amount to only 144,000 (cf. Luke 20.35, 1 Cor. 7.7). At the time of Antichrist there will be one particular error: he will forbid marrying (1 Tim. 4.1–3). The book of Daniel hints at this also by saying that the future Antichrist will not be married ("Neither shall he regard . . . the desire of women", 11.37). It is absolutely impossible that there will be only 144,000 Christians who neither worship idols nor follow evil doctrines. Since 14.4 is an explanation, it must mean simply what it clearly says and therefore needs no interpretation.

(2) "These are they that follow the Lamb whithersoever he goeth"—This verse does not speak of the past, it instead points to the present and the future. They are closest to the Lord, serving Him as His bodyguard.

(3) "These were purchased from among men, to be the first-fruits unto God and unto the Lamb"—They are men, yet they are purchased from among men. In Leviticus we are told that there are three different stages in reaping: the

first fruits (23.17), the harvest (23.22), and the gleaning (23.22). The farmer reaps when the wheat is ripened. He gathers into the garner what he cuts: he does not leave the wheat in the field. Thus, the time of rapture is in a sense decided by men and not by God. The reaping comes after ripening. The first fruits are Christians who mature first, hence are taken first.

14.5 The words of their mouths reveal what is in their hearts. These are the same descriptions concerning our Lord, but they are now applied also to the 144,000.

It should be pointed out, in conclusion, that this portion of Scripture does not exclude women from among the 144,000. It must be remembered that the Bible usually numbers only the men. For example, although a great number of women came out of Egypt and ate manna in the wilderness, God only counted the men but not the women. Moreover, though Dinah was Jacob's daughter, the nation of Israel had only twelve tribes. Yet neither does this portion of the Bible mean that there are only this number of people among the first group raptured. It simply demonstrates that there will be people such as these in the first group.

14.6,7 (cf. with v.8)   "THE FIRST ANGEL"

14.6 "Another angel"—He is different from the "another angel" spoken of in 7.2 that points to the Lord.

"Eternal good tidings"—The eternal gospel or good tidings is different from the gospel of grace. From the description which follows (14.7), it can be concluded that this eternal gospel is for the purpose of inducing people to worship the Creator. The eternal gospel preaches not God's redemption but His creation. It does not call man to worship the Lamb but to worship God. It does not proclaim the grace of God, only His judgment. It exhorts people to give glory to God.

Those meant by the phrases "them that dwell on the earth" and "every nation and tribe and tongue and people" (14.6) are not the same. The first refers to that special class of people from among the second—those who are especially related to the earth and who love worldly things most dearly. The future kingdom of Antichrist will only be as big as the Roman Empire, yet its influence will reach every nation and tribe and tongue and people. The words "them that dwell on the earth" may allude to those who dwell within the Roman Empire.

The gospel presented at this juncture is not proclaimed to cause people to believe in the Lord Jesus and be saved; instead, it is to teach them to worship God and not the image of the beast.

How do the sheep mentioned in Matthew 25.34–40 know to treat our Lord's little brother well (see v.40)? It is due to the influence of the proclamation of the angel here.

14.7 "Fear God"—It is clear in the Old Testament that to be kind to others is indicative of the people's fearing God. Since the hour of judgment is come, let people fear God and give glory to Him.

Heaven is damaged at the fourth trumpet. The earth is damaged at the first trumpet; the sea, at the second; and the fountains of all waters, at the third.

14.8 "A SECOND ANGEL"

To what does this city of Babylon refer? To Babylon or to Rome? The Babylon in chapter 17 is a mystery and has reference to Rome as a religious system. The Babylon here in 14.8 is also connected with the Roman religious system, for the description concerning both is the same. So that the second angel notifies the world that Babylon is fallen; that is to say, the Roman religious system is defeated. From this we can infer that the big harvest follows upon the defeat of the Roman religious system.

"The wine of the wrath of her fornication" signifies the oppression which the Roman religious system will mete out to people. To those unfaithful to the Lord will she give the wine of fornication; and to the faithful will she give the wine of wrath. Wine speaks of that which bewilders people.

The Roman religious system will be revived, but she will also be totally destroyed.

14.9-12 "THE THIRD ANGEL"

14.10 The purpose of the word in this verse is to inform people who behave themselves according to 14.9 that they will receive punishment from God. The punishment is two-fold: (1) to receive "the wine of the wrath of God"—the wrath of God, as shown in chapter 15, which is temporary; and (2) to be "tormented with fire and brimstone in the presence . . . of the Lamb"—this is to say that they have no hope of receiving grace. To be tormented in the presence of the angels simply means that they are put into the lake of fire by the angels.

14.11 This verse shows that after one has entered the lake of fire there is no more opportunity to repent; yet neither is he therefore annihilated. The saints need no sleep in heaven, but neither can the sinners sleep in the lake of fire.

14.12 agrees with 13.10. "Keep the commandments

of God" are words that refer especially to the first and second commandments. This is the time for the saints to be patient.

14.13 "BLESSED ARE THE DEAD"

"From henceforth" means from the time when the worship of the image of the beast is forced upon men. Through death people can thus escape the persecution of the beast. "Who die in the Lord"—these must be Christians. Here the Spirit is not called by the title the seven Spirits of God but by the name of the (Holy) Spirit, because "the seven Spirits" is a term which is particularly connected with God's judgment whereas "the Holy Spirit" is the term especially related to the church.

The effect of our work cannot go before God ahead of us, though the work of Christ does precede us so as to make us acceptable before God. Our works shall follow us that we may receive reward from God.

14.14-16 "AND REAP"

14.14 The phrase "a white cloud" fits perfectly with the words in 1 Thessalonians 4.16,17. "Like unto a son of man" shows that this word is spoken to the church (see 1.13).

The words "having on his head a golden crown" reveal that He is already glorified. A sharp sickle is indicated for quick reaping. In Matthew 13.37 the Lord is identified as the sower; at His second coming He will be the reaper.

14.15 An angel delivers the order of God to the Lord, for the Lord is here taking the place of a servant. In

Matthew 9.38 the Lord is recorded as distinctly declaring that God is the Lord of the harvest, so the Lord is presented as a sent one here in 14.15.

Never in the Bible does harvesting carry with it a bad connotation. Unlike figs on the fig trees, wheat cannot remain too long in the field after the ripening. It must be reaped. The first mentioning of harvest in Scriptures is found in Genesis 8.22. Being a harvest, it is a token of God's blessing. When the Lord speaks of harvest (John 4.35), He too means it well. According to Matthew 3.12 wheat is to be gathered into the garner. According to Leviticus 23, the first fruits of the harvest are to be brought into the house of God (see also Ex. 23.19, 34.26). This typifies how at the first rapture Christians are to be caught up to the throne of God. To gather wheat into the garner, therefore, signifies those Christians who are caught up to the air to meet the Lord, for the garner is built between the field and the home—the field being the world (Matt. 13.38) and the home being heaven. Consequently, the Christians in the harvest are taken up to the air which lies between heaven and the world.

The harvesting mentioned in Matthew 13.37–43 is for the purpose of gathering what the Lord has earlier sown. Since He sows only the good seed, He shall reap only what is good. In Mark 4.26–29 it is said that God comes to reap, for the time of harvest is come. Just as the first fruits are holy, so too is the rest (Rom. 11.16). The first fruits spoken of in Revelation 14.1–5 being so good, the harvest stated in 14.14–16 must also be good: for the harvest does not refer to the judgment of sinners.

"Ripe" can also be translated "become dry" (mg.). Unripened wheat cannot be harvested; neither can unmatured Christians be raptured. The first fruits ripen first, and therefore they can leave the world earlier. Christians who love the world need to "become dry" or scorched by the world before they will cease loving it.

14.15,16 According to Matthew 13.39 the reapers are angels. Hence the sickle mentioned here in 14.15,16 is that which is in the hands of the angels. It is a mystical sickle.

As the Lord receives us, we shall be raptured. We are "to stand before the Son of man" (Luke 21.36).

14.17–20 "GATHER THE VINTAGE"

Observe that 14.14–16 speaks of harvest and 14.17–20 speaks of vintage. Throughout the Bible wheat is always a representation of Christians whereas fig trees usually point to the Jews. Now sometimes grapes can stand for the wicked of the nations. And the reasons for concluding this are as follows:

(1) The Lord has not said that He himself is the grape; instead, He says that He is the true vine. The Lord Jesus is the true vine, and Christians are its branches. With the life of Christ in them, Christians are to produce heavenly grapes. By contrast, though, the earthly grapes before us here must refer to Antichrist and his followers.

(2) The vintage mentioned here takes place following the harvest. And hence after the good ones are taken, what remains must be bad.

(3) Judging by chapter 19.18, the grapes cited here should be those wicked people who oppose Christ.

(4) The Old Testament likewise sometimes gives a bad connotation to grapes (see Deut. 32.32).

(5) Since blood comes out from the wine press (14.19–

20), these grapes that are crushed cannot have any good meaning about them.

(6) From reading Joel 3.13 and Isaiah 63.1–6 we can assume that treading the winepress represents the wrath of God, and hence God's judgment.

Therefore, the passage in 14.14–16 shows the consequence of the wheat whereas 14.17–20 shows that of the tares.

After the Christians are raptured, God will send angels to gather the tares. The sickle is therefore also sharp.

As wheat is ripened, it dries up. But the grape as it ripens becomes more juicy. The wheat and the grape are just the opposite to each other. As the wheat dies to the earth it ripens. But the more the vine draws from the earth, the more the grapes are ripened. Since the nations have become more worldly and have extracted more and more from the world, their iniquity is full, and the time for their judgment is therefore come.

Note that 14.16 says "Cast his sickle *upon* the earth", which means only a swift cutting. But 14.19 says "cast his sickle *into* the earth", as though meaning to uproot the whole thing. This too shows the difference between the reaping of wheat and the gathering of grapes.

A "winepress" is a kind of stonepress into which the grapes are put and juice is squeezed out from them. It involves pain and suffering.

This passage of 14.17–20 will be fulfilled at the appearing of the Lord Jesus on earth. It coincides with 19.15 in that (1) the phrase "without the city" in 14.20 proves that it must be outside the city of Jerusalem (chapters 15 and 16 are supplementary to the seventh trumpet), and (2) the phrase "the bridles of the horses" in 14.20 agrees with 19.14 wherein we are told that the Lord and His heavenly hosts will ride on horses.

"A thousand and six hundred furlongs" (14.20). According to 16.16 this war will be fought in Har-Magedon, and Isaiah 63.1 tells us that it will begin from Bozrah. Measuring the distance from Bozrah to Magedon, it is 1600 furlongs (about 200 miles). The battle of Har-Magedon comes at a time when the feet of the Lord shall stand upon the Mount of Olives, which will be cleft into two so as to allow the Jews who are fleeing from the persecution of Antichrist to escape (Zech. 14.4,5). Then shall the Lord fight with Antichrist and destroy him (Rev. 19.17–21).

The kingdom of God will be ushered in, not through the preaching of the Gospel, but by the shedding of blood. The church must wait until the return of the Lord for the final arrival of the kingdom.

Isaiah 34.1–8 describes the slaughtering in Bozrah.

After these things shall come the kingdom of God. Following the harvest and the vintage there is the feast of the tabernacles which serves as a type of the millennial kingdom.

PART EIGHT

POURING SEVEN BOWLS

Pouring Seven Bowls
(15.1–16.21)

Chapters 15 and 16 do not follow 14.17–20 chronologically for the latter agrees with 19.15.

15.1 "THE LAST SEVEN PLAGUES"

In 12.1 the term used is "a great sign"; here in 15.1 the term is a "sign . . . great and marvelous . . ."

15.2-4 DOXOLOGY

15.2 "A sea of glass"—This has been mentioned once before in 4.6, though neither people nor fire are seen. Here in 15.2 both people as well as fire are mentioned. Since the sea of glass spoken of in 4.6 is before the throne, that is to say, in heaven, the people on the sea of glass mentioned here in 15.2 must have therefore been taken to heaven. So that this portion of Scripture tells us of a people who have passed through the Great Tribulation and who have also seen the beast, his image, and his number. Inasmuch as 14.14–16 shows us how they are raptured from earth, 15.2 discloses how they are received in heaven.

15.3 Why do they sing the song of Moses as well as the song of the Lamb? It should be noted that had they worshiped the image of the beast they would have violated

the law of Moses and the commandment of God. But they
have not worshiped the image of the beast: therefore, they
sing the song of Moses. He who commands them not to
worship idols is Moses, and so they sing the song of Moses.
He who gives them strength not to worship idols is the
Lamb, and hence they sing the song of the Lamb. What
they sing is clearly recorded in 15.3,4. It is evident that it is
not the same song of Moses that was sung at the time of
Exodus 15.

The first clause in the song refers to the works of God,
while the second refers to the ways of God. Works are
outward acts, but ways are inward principles. "Lord God"
is a name which shows how God is related to man. "King of
the ages" can also be translated as "King of the nations"
(mg.). "Righteous" pertains to principle, whereas "true"
pertains to promise.

15.4 The word "holy" describes God's nature; the
words "righteous acts" describe the ways of God's working.

15.5-8 "THE TEMPLE OF THE TABERNACLE"

15.5 "The temple of the tabernacle" is in heaven, yet
it is not permanent since it is described as a *tabernacle*
temple. The tabernacle of Moses was made after the
heavenly pattern (Heb. 8.5). After the holy temple was
built by Solomon, the tabernacle passed away. So in like
manner, when in eternity the Lamb shall become the
temple, even this temple of the tabernacle in heaven will
pass away.

15.6 These seven angels are priestly angels since they
wear priestly garments. Perhaps they serve God in the
heavenly temple. According to the order of the Old

Testament, the drink offering is poured out before the burning of the sacrifice. Their action seems to follow such an order.

15.8 This verse means that hereafter no one may enter the temple of God to intercede. At that hour the wrath of God is beyond the point of return (cf. Lam. 3.44).

16.1–21 "THE SEVEN BOWLS"

The plagues in bowl 1 to bowl 6 seem to be quite similar to the plagues in trumpet 1 to trumpet 6; the only difference lies in their intensities. The six bowls re-enact the plagues of the six trumpets, but with much greater severity. Since the seventh trumpet includes all seven bowls, the weight of woe must be tremendously heavy.

16.2 "The first bowl"

The men who suffer in this plague are those that have upon themselves the mark of the beast and who worship his image. This sore is similar to that which the poor man Lazarus once had. It is not cured even to death. One of the ten plagues of Egypt was this boil. Job was attacked by sore boils, so too, Hezekiah once had this sore. The Philistines at one time were punished with a sore. God sometimes uses the sore to judge people (Deut. 28.15,27). Since these men bear the mark of the beast, they are also given a sore by God as their mark.

The first trumpet only hurts the trees and grass on earth, but the first bowl hurts people directly.

16.3   "The Second Bowl"

The plague in the second bowl is more severe than that of the first one since it is larger in scope and becomes blood as of a dead man. Maritime business comes to a complete stop (Ps. 105.29; Is. 50.2).

16.4–7   "The Third Bowl"

In the third trumpet only the third part of the waters becomes bitter to the taste; but now all of the water is turned into blood which cannot be drunk. The reason why God gives them blood to drink is because they have persecuted the Christians as well as His prophets.

In 16.5 there is an angel who is in charge of all the waters.

In 1.8 and 4.8 God is called the one "who is and who was and who is to come, the Almighty"; but after both 11.17 and 16.5 the phrase "who is to come" is no longer used. Thus it shows that the return of the Lord must be after the time of chapter 4 but before that of 11.17.

In 16.7 the word "righteous" pertains to God's principles, while "true" pertains to God's promises.

16.8,9   "The Fourth Bowl"

In the fourth trumpet the third part of the heavenly bodies is smitten with darkness, but now the sun scorches men with fire (see also Luke 21.25). Isaiah predicts that "the inhabitants of the earth are burned" (24.6). Most likely they will be burned by the heat of the sun (Is. 42.25; Deut. 32.24; Mal. 4.1). People remember how they suffer but fail to ponder why they suffer. They take no heed of the message proclaimed by the angel as recorded in 14.6,7.

16.10,11 "The Fifth Bowl"

This is related to the angel of the abyss in the fifth trumpet. The pain mentioned in verse 10 is due to the sore of the first bowl and the scorching of the sun in the fourth bowl. In addition to the plagues of the former bowls is this terrible darkness.

16.12–16 "The Sixth Bowl"

Note that 16.12 is the sixth bowl, while 16.13–16 is an interpolated vision.

16.12 "The great river, the river Euphrates"—The land which God had promised to the children of Israel extended from the river of Egypt to the great river Euphrates (Gen. 15.18). History also tells us that during the most prosperous period of the ancient Roman Empire, her boundary reached the great Euphrates River. In the future there will arise two confederacies; one of the West, taking the Mediterranean Sea as its center with the territory covered by the ancient Roman Empire as its domain (including England, France, the northern coast of Africa, Spain, Portugal, Romania, Czechoslovakia, Greece, and even reaching to India and the Persian boundary); one of the East, with Soviet Russia as its center, and including the Persians, the Cushites, the Turks, and so forth. It may also include China, Japan, Afghanistan, etc.*

---

* In his latter years the author spoke of three confederacies arising in the world before the coming of Christ; namely, the so-called revived Roman Empire or the confederacy of the West, the Northern confederacy as outlined in Ezekiel 38.1–6, and the confederacy of the Kings of the East as alluded to in Revelation 16.12.—*Translator*

The river Euphrates is wide and its current swift. But at the pouring of the sixth bowl its water is dried up, thus easily crossed.

16.13 "Unclean spirits"—These unclean spirits are in direct opposition to the Holy Spirit. The word "frogs" symbolizes mischievousness.

16.13,14 The gathering together of the kings of the whole world has no other reason than to war. We can see how they are instigated by the spirits of demons to war. Eventually they will be destroyed by the appearing of the Lord.

16.15 Here are still some words spoken to Christians. "Behold, I come as a thief" are words spoken by the Lord to His church. These words may be spoken to those mentioned in Revelation 14.14–16 who are waiting to be harvested, or they may be spoken to the Christians who are left to be gleaned. The vintage spoken of in 14.17–20 is the same as the battle of Har-Magedon spoken of in 16.16. Therefore, 16.15 may refer either to the harvest of Christians before the battle of Har-Magedon or to Christians waiting to be gleaned after the harvest is gathered and before the battle is fought.

16.16 "Har-Magedon"—Magedon is the name of a place, while "Har" means mountain. Hence it is the mountain of Magedon, the same as Jezreel cited in the Old Testament.

16.17–21 "The Seventh Bowl"

16.17 The words "It is done" may also be translated "It is enough". "The air" is where Satan once ruled.

Perhaps there is yet some residual satanic influence in the air, hence this final punishment.

16.18 "A great earthquake"—See Ezekiel 38.20.

16.19 "The great city" means Jerusalem. The Babylon cited here points to the actual Babylon (14.8 "fallen, fallen is Babylon" happens before the battle of Har-Magedon and is synchronized with 17.16–19. "Babylon the great" is the actual Babylon whose fall is complete after the battle of Har-Magedon, and so it coincides with the latter half of chapter 18). The verses in 14.8 and 16.19 give a sketch concerning Babylon while chapters 17 and 18 furnish the details.

16.20 Every island flees away and all the mountains vanish. How very severe must be this earthquake! According to the Psalms, there will still be islands and mountains during the millennium (Ps. 72.3,10; 97.1).

16.21 A Greek talent is about 56 English pounds, while a Jewish talent is equivalent to approximately 114 English pounds. Along with the great earthquake there is great hail.

PART NINE

BABYLON AND HER DESTRUCTION

Babylon and Her Destruction
(17.1–20.6)

The long section from 17.1 to 18.24 is best to be taken as one single chapter. Please note also that 18.1–3 serves as transitional words, since they conclude what has been spoken previously and commence what is next going to be said; for these verses mention the following three things:

(1) "By the wine of the wrath of her fornication all the nations are fallen"—only chapter 17 mentions this (17.2);

(2) "The merchants of the earth waxed rich by the power of her wantonness"—only chapter 18 mentions this (18.11,15); and

(3) "The kings of the earth committed fornication with her"—both chapters 17 and 18 speak about this (17.2, 18.9).

The word "Babylon" comes from "Babel": It is recorded in Genesis 10 and 11 that Nimrod built the city of Babel in the land of Shinar. It was he who tried to protect himself by his own strength. The origin of the tower of Babel is found in Genesis 11.1–4. God confounded the language of the people and scattered them abroad upon the face of all the earth. Hence the city was called "Babel" (11.9). "Babel" or "Babylon" simply means "confusion". Idol-worship began there, and it stood in opposition to God. The city grew larger and larger until it reached its golden age at the time of Nebuchadnezzar. Due to the unfaithfulness of the children of Israel, God delivered them into the hands of Nebuchadnezzar the king of Babylon.

In the days of Daniel, King Nebuchadnezzar dreamed of a huge image: and by interpretation he himself was the image's head of gold, the most prosperous period in the history of Babylon; then Medo-Persia (the image's arms of silver) destroyed Babylon, and the city became desolate. Later on, Greece (the image's belly of brass) destroyed Medo-Persia; and Greece was in turn destroyed by Rome (the image's legs of iron). Babylon was therefore the first kingdom, while Rome was the last kingdom. And these four kingdoms oppressed the Jews. Three kingdoms have already passed away, but Rome has continued on. The ten toes of the image have yet to appear. Now just as Babylon had greatly worshiped idols and deeply hated the Jews, so has Rome.

Rome was not only politically a city, it was also a center of religion. In the city of Rome were to be found many Christians, yet Rome hated Christians the most. Not until the fourth century after Christ did Constantine the Great accept Christianity and encourage his people to do the same. With the result that Christianity became the official religion of Rome. At the same time, though, the center of politics shifted from Rome to Constantinople. Rome itself became subject to the rule of Constantinople and remained that way until the sixth century. At the time of Leo a general council was held at Constantinople wherein idol-worship was condemned as heretical and illegal. Rome opposed this, and she broke with Constantinople. Thus were formed the Eastern Roman Church (the Greek Orthodox Church) and the Western Roman Church (the Roman Catholic Church). The influence of the Eastern Roman Church began to wane, but that of the Western Roman Church increased steadily. A great number of Christians suffered death at the hands of the Roman Catholic Church.

According to Revelation 17 and 18 the Roman Catholic Church will experience tremendous growth in the future, far exceeding that of the past. Her influence will be enormous. But when Antichrist shall arise and set up his image as an object of worship, he with his ten subordinate kings shall destroy the Roman Church. Nevertheless, with the passing of Rome religious, Rome political will still continue. She will make the Mediterranean Sea a center of her influence. Three and a half years later, God will destroy Rome political.

Why is it that chapters 17 and 18 do not mention Rome plainly, but use Babylon instead? Because John lived under the reign of Rome. If he should have plainly written of Rome, his writing might not have been able to be circulated—yet not that John was afraid to write explicitly, but that the Holy Spirit intended to have it hidden. Nevertheless, the same Spirit is concerned lest people take Babylon as being literal. So in Revelation 17.5 He declares:

(1) "Mystery, Babylon the Great"—Being a mystery, it must be spiritual and not literal in its interpretation. For instance, if in 11.8 Jerusalem had been plainly mentioned, the Jews would have immediately risen up in arms. So that a spiritualized form of writing is here used.

(2) By saying Babylon the Great instead of simply Babylon, it intimates that this Babylon is much greater than the actual Babylon of the past. Such a rendering thus helps the reader to know that Babylon is not to be taken as Babylon literally but is to be understood as standing for Rome.

Why Babylon Here Points to Rome

(1) Only one city in the world is built on seven hills or

mountains, and that is the city of Rome. Rome historically is called the seven-hilled city (cf. 17.9).

(2) "Fallen" in 17.10 has reference, as we have indicated before, to violent death. Some were murdered, some committed suicide. At the time of John's writing this book, the king who was then living must have been a Roman Caesar.

(3) Besides the king of Rome there was none else at that time who reigned over the kings of the earth (cf. 17.18).

In What Respects Babylon Resembles Rome

(1) Babylon was the first nation which broke through to the Jewish holy land and entered the holy place. But so did Rome.

(2) Babylon, as we have said, means confusion. How very greatly confused was Rome also—and still is! She mixed up the church with the country, the church with the world, law with grace, the traditions of men with the word of God, the pagans with the Christians, Judaism with Christianity, God's promises to the church with His promises to the Jews, the carnal with the spiritual, the earthly with the heavenly, the present rejection with the future glory. In fact, she is the center of all mixtures. How extensive is her confusion indeed!

(3) The church fathers themselves regarded Rome as Babylon. Tertullian noted that Babylon was Rome. Jerome said, "When I dwelt in Babylon and resided within the walls of the scarlet adulteress, and had the freedom of Rome, I undertook a work concerning the Holy Spirit, which I proposed to ascribe to the Bishop of that city." And Augustine said, "Babylon is a former Rome, and Rome a

later Babylon." *

(4) Some prominent Romish writers such as Robert Bellarmine, Cesare Baronius, Jacques Bossuet, and Hug have also admitted that Babylon meant Rome. Bellarmine, for example, wrote this: "Moreover, John in the Apocalypse everywhere calls Rome Babylon." **

There is a school of thought which maintains that Babylon points only to political Rome, not to religious Rome. This concept, though, is erroneous. If Babylon only refers to political Rome, why should "fallen" be mentioned twice in 14.8 and 16.19? For the event represented by the word "fallen" in 14.8 happens before the setting up of the image of the beast; therefore it is an event occurring during the first three and a half years. But the "fallen" ("fell") told about in 16.19 takes place at the time of the seventh bowl, that is to say, after the setting up of the image of the beast. Hence there must be two different aspects of Babylon in view. This fits in perfectly with both religious Rome (since "Babylon" means confusion, and this confusion prevails in the realm of religion) and political Rome (since "Rome" in Hebrew means "the one who exalts himself", and how she exalts herself in opposition to God).

"Mystery, Babylon the Great" alludes to the religion of Rome. The reasons for this view are:

(1) "The great harlot that sitteth upon many waters" (17.1). This harlot is a city. Since the city of Rome is never built on many waters (there is only one river in the city of Rome), this harlot cannot be applied to political Rome.

(2) "The seven heads are seven mountains, on which the woman sitteth" (17.9). As indicated earlier, Rome is built

---

* Robert Govett, *The Apocalypse Expounded*, London: Chas. J. Thynne, 1920, p. 442.—*Translator*
** Govett, *Ibid.*, p. 442.—*Translator*

on seven mountains and she is called the seven-hilled city. Since this seven-hilled city points to political Rome, the harlot here who sits on the seven mountains cannot herself be representative of political Rome but must stand for religious Rome that sits above political Rome.

(3) "And when I saw her, I wondered with a great wonder" (17.6). Should this woman point to political Rome, where is the wonder or surprise to be found in that? She instead must be religious Rome, and hence the amazement. It is not at all surprising for the nations to persecute Christians; but for the Roman Church to persecute Christians, this is really astounding.

(4) The "fornication" mentioned in 17.2 cannot be applied to something physical, it has to be a reference to something doctrinal in nature. A physical city is unable to commit physical fornication; so that what is meant here must have application to religious Rome.

(5) Political Rome controls the kings of the earth, hence it is not possible for political Rome to commit fornication with them. The great harlot in 17.2 is without doubt religious Rome.

Nevertheless, Babylon also has reference to political Rome, for the following reasons:

(1) According to 17.16 the end of the woman comes when she is burned by the beast (Antichrist) and ten horns (ten subordinate kings). But in 18.8 she is judged by God. For this reason, 17.16 has reference to the religious aspect whereas 18.8 has reference to the political aspect.

(2) In 18.7 it reads: "She saith in her heart, I sit a queen"; but by the time of 17.16 she is already dethroned by the beast and the ten kings. How, then, can it still be said in 18.7 that she sits a queen? This is possible only because one speaks of religious Rome and the other of political Rome.

(3) Chapter 17 is largely symbolic, while the latter half of chapter 18 is almost entirely literal. The angel explains to John what is shown in chapter 17 because it *is* allegorical; but the second part of chapter 18 needs no interpretation since it is not symbolic.

(4) After 8.13 records "Woe, woe, woe", there in fact do come three woes shortly thereafter. Similarly, when 18.2 mentions "fallen, fallen", there must be two fallings to come; one, the fall of political Rome; the other, the fall of religious Rome.

(5) There are two Jerusalems referred to in this book: one is on earth and one, in heaven. Likewise, there are to be found the two aspects of Rome in this book: one which is political and one religious. These two are distinguishable but not separable.

17.1 This begins the narration of the things that are to occur after the pouring out of the seven bowls. Is it not interesting that one of the seven angels who has the seven bowls signifies the New Jerusalem to John in direct contrast with what is said in 17.1? Before the harlot is judged, God cannot show forth the wife of the Lamb.

The phrase "many waters" here in 17.1 indicates "Peoples, and multitudes, and nations, and tongues" (see 17.15). The harlot sits upon peoples and multitudes and nations and tongues. In other words, the influence of Rome extends throughout the entire world. How the Romish system frequently styles itself as the mistress and mother of all churches.

Why does God call this woman a harlot? Because she communicates and commingles with the world. She has so broadened the communion of the saints as to hold intercourse with the world. What she gains is worldly pleasure and earthly glory. She has become savorless salt. A harlot is one who commits fornication without the due process of marriage. An adulteress is a woman who commits fornication *after* being married. God therefore calls her a harlot, since a harlot is a woman who commits fornication *before* marriage; thus signifying that God has never recognized the relationship between the Roman Church and Christ. Like a harlot, the Roman Church has not kept her virginity for Christ.

This woman is called a "*great* harlot": Had the Roman Catholic Church observed Matthew 5–7, she could not be great—she could only develop into a "little flock" (Luke 12.32). Her testimony would simply be that the world is rebellious and that Christ shall come again to judge it. Her being "great" is exactly what the Lord predicted in Matthew 13.32. In this connection we need to read Genesis 1 which states that "the earth brought forth grass, herbs yielding seed after their kind, and trees bearing fruit, wherein is the seed thereof, after their kind" (v.12). Yet Matthew 13 records the Lord Jesus as saying this: "When it is grown, it is greater than the herbs, and becometh a tree" (v.32). Hence the greatness here described in Revelation is the greatness of a harlot. Please observe that the Romish pope is greater than an emperor. An emperor can only control a man's body, but a pope can control a man's soul, yes, even that of the emperor's. Now such a situation is not at all normal for the church on earth.

17.2 "With whom the kings of the earth committed fornication"—By way of explanation please consider the following:

(1) In order to please the kings of the earth, the Roman Church was willing to baptize them as long as they wished to be baptized. Thus, she auctioned away the principles of Christ and the word of God.

(2) She made the church co-extensive with the state. Christianity became the state religion of Rome. Anyone who was born a Roman could be a Christian. Normally the church was smaller than the state, but now she became equally as big.

(3) The Church joined to herself the political powers of kings and rulers. The foremost sin of fornication she can commit is to force Christianity on the people by means of the powers of kings and emperors. This was done not only by Rome but also by many other nations. The result was to make merely nominal Christians out of people.

To commit fornication with the kings of the earth is said to be, interpretively speaking, the Roman Church's direct relationship with them. But the verse, "and they that dwell in the earth were made drunken with the wine of her fornication", speaks of her indirect relationship with the people on earth. Wine here signifies heresies. The Romish Church has caused people on earth to lose their self-determination and to become foolish through heretical doctrines. On the one hand she has taught that by giving a little money and by making confession to a priest a person's sin may be forgiven, but on the other hand she has failed to instruct people how they ought to live a holy life. She allows them to indulge in worldly pleasures. Indeed, this wine of her fornication has made the whole world drunk. It is quite true that without religion no one could live on earth. For this reason, the Roman Church is most palatable to the taste of the world. She disregards spiritual reality on the one hand, yet on the other uses all sorts of religious rituals to create emotional comforts as well as glowing expectation within the hearts of the people.

So has been the Church of Rome, and so shall she be revived in the future. For instance, in China there are only about 300,000 to 400,000 Protestants, but there are more than 2,000,000 Roman Catholics.* Furthermore, once a Roman Catholic, one dies a Roman Catholic. Several big denominations in the United States had no increase during one year, whereas the Roman Catholics added several millions to their record.

17.3 "Wilderness" may be interpreted spiritually, for the world is referred to in Scripture as a wilderness (Ps. 107.33,34); or it may be interpreted literally, since the vicinity of Rome itself has been called a "marble wilderness" by some.**

"A woman sitting upon a scarlet-colored beast"—This beast represents the Roman Empire, for the seven heads and ten horns are merely part of it; it also points to Antichrist, because even though he is the eighth head he nevertheless possesses all the villainy of the other seven as well as the powers of the ten horns. God looks upon Antichrist as just a wild beast. Moreover, He looks upon this woman as a harlot, for she is not as irrationally vicious as a wild beast, though she abandons her rationality and acts a harlot.

"A woman sitting upon . . . a beast"—This speaks of the union of the Roman Church with the Roman state. How this woman has made use of the state! If a local magistrate had offended a Roman Catholic priest, the pope might have issued an interdict upon the city, prohibiting the celebration of mass and thus stirring up the people against their magistrate. Or if the Roman Church had wished for any action to be taken against some people, she would not have acted directly; instead, she would have

---

* These statistics refer back to the early 1930's.—*Translator*
** Govett, *op. cit.,* p. 428.—*Translator*

instigated the Roman state to act. The woman's influence is as great as that of the beast, because she rides on the beast.

The color of the beast is red as that of the dragon is red. This indicates that this beast comes out of the dragon; therefore, it is the same as the dragon.

"Full of names of blasphemy"—This is different from the words of blasphemy. The words "names of blasphemy" mean calling oneself with the names used of God. How the Roman caesars were accustomed to employing divine titles!

17.4 "Purple"—This is the color adopted in the Roman Empire as the symbol of honor and power. For example, a Roman senator had a broad strip of purple on the breast, while a knight had a narrow strip of it. The emperor wore a purple robe. For the woman to be thus arrayed in purple means that she is in possession of earthly glory (note that the rich man cited in Luke 16.19 wore a robe of purple).

Purple is not a basic color since it is the combination of blue and red colors. Blue is the heavenly color, but red is the earthly (for note that the Biblical place-name Edom means red, and therefore this color denotes that which is earthly). Hence purple is the blending of heaven and earth.

Scarlet is the color of Rome—" 'I caused this inquiry to be made of an intelligent gentleman who had passed much time in Rome, without his knowing my design,' said Barnes. 'What would strike a stranger on visiting Rome, or what would be likely particularly to arrest his attention as remarkably there?' And he unhesitatingly replied, 'The scarlet color.' " * Scarlet is the special color of the ecclesiastical cardinals as well as the popes. The cardinals are so called since their dresses, their hats, their cloaks, and their

---

* Govett, *op. cit.*, p. 430.—*Translator*

stockings are always of scarlet. In the case of the pope, even the inner lining of his cloak is scarlet; and the costume of his bodyguard is also scarlet. Whenever the pope travels, he is welcomed with decorations of scarlet color.

"And decked with gold and precious stone and pearls"— All these things represent the truths of God. The Roman Church, like this woman, adorns herself with these outwardly (cf. 1 Peter 3.3, 1 Tim. 2.9); yet her real condition is most abnormal in the sight of God.

"Having in her hand a golden cup full of abominations" —This woman has no crown on her head for she is not a genuine queen, neither does she hold a staff in her hand since she is not supposed to possess any earthly authority. Instead she has in her hand a golden cup full of abominations, which speaks of her seducing power. Her victory is gained not by any direct authority, but through her seductive influence.

A metal was once struck by the pope in which a woman was holding in her hand a golden cup; and the caption read: "She sits upon the universe"! Unconsciously, the Roman Church acknowledges herself as that woman.

17.5 "And upon her forehead a name written, Mystery, Babylon the Great"—She is a mystery, and yet this mystery is written on her forehead for everyone to read. This implies that whoever has an eye can perceive the meaning of this mystery.

God recognized Jerusalem as the center of worship (religious) as well as the center of earthly dominion (political). The error of the Roman Church is to presume that God has established her in lieu of Jerusalem, thus making herself both a religious and political center. What Jerusalem is rightfully to be in the millennial kingdom is what the Roman Church has today already assumed.

"The mother of the harlots"—Being herself the great harlot, all that come out of this woman are harlots. These are the state churches, since their institutional systems are similar to that of Rome. Any church group that is united with the world is a small harlot. (For example, membership is not based on regeneration, but is granted to any who pledge to give support financially; also, the qualification for taking communion or the Lord's Supper is membership instead of salvation; and so forth).

"Mother . . . of the abominations of the earth"—Abominations in Old Testament times always pointed to idols (see Deut. 7.25,26). The Roman Church is known for her idol-worshiping. She worships Mary, angels, apostles, saints, and so forth. Her split with Constantinople was over this matter of her idol-worshiping.

17.6 This verse tells us what this woman did prior to what she will even more intensely and cruelly do in the future. Notice carefully that this verse does not say that the woman herself shed the blood of the saints and of the martyrs of Jesus; it merely states that she was "drunken with [their] blood": The Roman Church never slays people with her own hands, she instead uses the authority of the Roman state to kill. Whereas she is the instigator, it is the Roman state that directly persecutes the Christians.

The word "saints" here includes also the Jews, for in the future not only those who have the testimony of Jesus but also those who are Jews will suffer persecution from the hand of the Roman Church.

John is surprised because the persecution of Christians comes from a people who profess to believe in Christ. How can he not wonder with a great wonder?

It should be noted that 17.1–6 records the vision John

saw; 17.7 begins the interpretation given by the angel. Consequently, the section found in 17.7–18 should be taken literally.

17.7 The angel is going to tell John the mystery of the seven heads and ten horns

17.8 The angel explains to John that the beast he saw has four stages of history; namely, the beast (1) was, (2) is not, (3) is about to come out of the abyss, and (4) will go into perdition.

In the book of Revelation this beast, as has been said, represents Antichrist as well as the Roman Empire. In this connection, though, it points to a man, not to a state. The reasons for this view are as follows:

(1) This beast "was"—How then can we say that the Roman Empire once existed earlier prior to the time of John?

(2) The beast "is not"—Yet neither can we say that the Roman Empire did not exist at John's time.

(3) The beast "is about to come up out of the abyss"—Abyss is the place where *the spirits* are imprisoned. How can we therefore say that the Roman Empire is about to come out of the abyss?

(4) The beast is "to go into perdition"—How, moreover, can we say that the political entity known as the Roman Empire will go into hell in the future?

Since, from this reasoning, this beast cannot apply to the Roman Empire, it must have reference to Antichrist.

"Was" shows that before the time of John there was such a person who once lived on earth.

"Is not" indicates that at John's time this man is not in the world since he must have died. The phrase "is not" is also used in Genesis 42.36–38 to indicate death.

"Is about to come up out of the abyss" reveals that he is now in the abyss but will come out of it, that is to say, he will be resuscitated.

"Go into perdition" discloses that he will not live forever on earth, neither can he rule forever, because his destiny will be that of being cast into the lake of fire (19.20, 20.10).

His being "was, and is not, and is about to come" is a clever counterfeiting of God "who is and who was and who is to come" (cf. 1.4,8; 4.8).

"And they that dwell on the earth shall wonder"—And this wonderment will eventually lead them to worship the beast (13.12). Only those whom God has chosen will be kept. All whose names have been written in the book of life from the foundation of the world will be preserved by God and kept from worshiping the beast.

17.9 is the same as 13.18; except that in 13.18 it says that the mind that has wisdom can count the number of the beast, whereas in 17.9 it states that the mind of wisdom is to know the heads of the beast.

The seven heads have double meaning; they point to (1) place, and (2) person.

(1) As to place, the seven heads are seven mountains. The heads of the earth are mountains, which also give the impression of strength or power (see Num. 21.20; Jer. 22.6; Amos 1.2, 9.3).

"Rome was in John's age usually called the seven-hilled city", said Dr. Woodworth. Many of the ancient Roman poets in their poetry proclaimed Rome as the seven-hilled city. Someone has noticed that for about five hundred years after the time of John, the Roman poets unanimously called Rome the seven-hilled city. There was once a Roman gold metal which showed a woman sitting on seven hills. Even the coin of Emperor Vespasian, as described by Captain

Smyth (*Roman Coins*, page 310), represented "Rome seated on seven hills; at the base Romulus and Remus suckled by the wolf; in front, the Tiber personified." *

The poet Horace once said, "The gods, who look with favour on the seven hills." And another poet Tibullus said this: "Ye bulls, feed on herbage of the seven hills."

Now the names of the seven hills are these: Aventine, Coelian, Esquiline, Capitoline, Palatine, Quirinal, and Viminal.

(2) As to person, these seven mountains are also seven kings, for kings are heads of the peoples. While the heads of the earth (that is, the mountains) are contemporary and continuous, the heads of the peoples are temporary and successive to one another. This double concept of head as being both of the earth and of the people may be demonstrated in one particular passage of Isaiah: "The head of Syria is Damascus, and the head of Damascus is Rezin" (7.8,9).

Some people interpret the seven kings as constituting seven forms of government. Such elucidation is against the rules of scriptural interpretation, as is seen in the following observations:

(1) The seven kings being already the angel's own explanation, they cannot be expounded in any other way.

(2) The Bible never uses a king to represent politics. Even classical writers do not employ such symbolism.

(3) The concept of a king is itself already the symbol of a form of government (he may represent either an absolute or a constitutional form of monarchy). How then can these kings stand for other forms of government?

(4) In spite of the finding by some of seven different

---

* Robert Govett, *The Apocalypse Expounded.* London: Chas. J. Thynne, 1920, p. 442.—*Translator*

forms of Roman government, the seven kings alluded to here succeed one another, whereas the seven forms of Roman government are not continuous but are intermittent.

(5) If the seven kings point to seven forms of government, what will the ten kings represent? Will they not stand for another ten forms of government? If so, Roman political history would have required 17 forms of government.

(6) 17.9 speaks of the woman sitting upon seven mountains. *Each* of the seven is a mountain; not that some are mountains and some are not. Similarly, therefore, the seven kings must all be kings.

(7) "Head" in the Scripture always has reference to person. The four heads mentioned in Daniel 7.6 represent four kings, not four forms of government. Why, then, should the seven kings in Revelation represent seven forms of government?

(8) If the kings have reference to various forms of government, then that of "Christian" emperors (such as Constantine the Great) must also be reckoned as numbering among the forms of government. But according to 12.3 the seven heads are located upon the dragon and hence all these heads belong to Satan. Can we say Christianity too belongs to Satan?

Yet some critics counter respond by saying that Rome had twelve caesars, with Domitian at the time of John already being the twelfth caesar. How can we therefore say that Rome has only seven kings? We may answer this by asking why it is that there are only seven specific churches cited in chapters 2 and 3? Obviously, the seven churches are chosen representatively. The same, too, in the matter of the seven kings.

Even so, some may still further argue that even if the seven kings may perhaps be selected on a representative basis, how is anyone to know which seven out of the twelve caesars are to be chosen? Our answer is that we may find them out by means of the following deductions:

(1) 13.1 states: "And upon his heads names of blasphemy"; since the seven heads all have names of blasphemy, these seven kings must be self-styled gods, demanding worship.

(2) The word "fallen" in 17.10 carries with it the idea of violent death (see 2 Sam. 1.19,25,27). All seven kings do indeed meet with violent death: Julius Caesar, Tiberius, Caligula, Claudius, and Nero—these five kings all assumed deity for themselves; they called for their people to worship them as gods; and all five died unnaturally, either by being murdered or by committing suicide.

Domitian was the sixth one. He was present during the time of John. He too deified himself, and was later murdered.

The seventh one is he who is yet to come. The Bible does not tell us how far apart time-wise the seventh is from the sixth; only that the seventh one will continue a little while (17.10) and later be killed (17.10; 13.3,14).

The interval between the sixth and the seventh one is filled by the reign of religious Rome. From the first to the sixth, also during the seventh and the eighth, political Rome is in power. But now it is currently religious Rome in place of political Rome.

After Zedekiah was taken captive into Babylon there was no king in Israel. A long interval passed before Christ was born. Likewise, after the destruction of Rome there will be an interval before Antichrist appears.

The whole world will be well prepared for the arrival of Antichrist. Hence, as soon as he appears on the scene he will be able to do much during the three and a half years.

The seventh king will have already prepared for the eighth one.

      17.11 This verse should be read together with 17.8, for just as 17.8 speaks of the four historical stages of the beast so does 17.11. According to 17.11 the four stages of the beast's history are denominated as (1) "was", (2) "is not", (3) "is of the seven", and (4) "goeth into perdition".

Since (1), (2) and (4) in 17.11 coincide with (1), (2) and (4) in 17.8, quite naturally (3) in 17.11 must also agree with (3) in 17.8. Thus, the beast must come out of the abyss.

Because he is said to be an eighth yet is also of the seven and because he comes out of the abyss, he must needs be one of the seven who is raised from death to be the eighth. Which one of the seven will he be?

(1) He cannot be the seventh since the seventh has yet to come to the world (17.10), whereas the beast has already been in the world before (17.8).

(2) He cannot be the sixth because the sixth was on earth when John lived, but this beast "is not" at the time of John (17.11).

Since he is neither the seventh nor the sixth, he must be one of the five. But which of the five is he? From 13.18 we recognize that he must be Nero.

The seventh is but a forerunner of Antichrist. The eighth is to use the body of the seventh. Eight is the number of resurrection; yet his resurrection is to be quite different from that of the Lord Jesus. For the Lord is himself resurrected, but the eighth is to be the reanimation ˉf a corpse with another soul.*

---

* This is *not* to be construed as teaching reincarnation. The Bible does not teach reincarnation, nor did the author ever subscribe to such an heretical doctrine. The specific interpretation given here relative to Antichrist serves

While the Lord Jesus was on earth the Jews chose a living caesar rather than the living Christ. After Christ was resurrected, people still refused to accept Him. The future Antichrist will be a resurrected caesar, and again people will receive him instead of the risen Christ.

17.12 The seven heads are seven kings, but so are the ten horns ten kings. Yet the heads and the horns are different.

(1) A horn is on the head; therefore, it is relatively smaller than the head. A head represents the entire reign of Rome while a horn stands for a subordinate king of Rome (such as a tetrarch or prince).

(2) There can be only one head at a time, and these heads succeed one another in reigning; but the ten horns can be ten subordinate kings ruling contemporaneously.

(3) Of the seven heads, one is yet to come; but of the ten horns, all are yet to come.

These horns or kings had received no kingdom as yet while John was living.

The ten kings shall receive authority simultaneously with the eighth.

Some suggest that the ten kings are a reference to ten kingdoms. But such an interpretation is not valid for the following reasons:

(1) Ten kings is the explanation of the angel, so there should be no further interpretation.

(2) 17.12 and 17.17 will not make sense if these ten kings are re-interpreted as being ten kingdoms.

---

only as the exception which goes to prove the rule of *no* reincarnation—just as the image of the beast having breath and the ability to speak (see 13.14,15 above) is the exception which proves the rule of *no* image having breath or speaking.—*Translator*

(3) Since the beast is a person, the ten kings must likewise be persons.

These ten kings are different from the kings of the earth because:

(1) The kings of the earth exist prior to and also at the time of the ten kings.

(2) The kings of the earth commit fornication with the great harlot, but the ten kings have never been united with the great harlot. On the contrary, they later on destroy her (17.16).

17.13 The beast cannot refer to the pope, for never have ten kings ever given their power to a pope. Nor can the beast be an allusion to any of the former Roman emperors, since, again, no ten kings have ever surrendered their power to any former Roman emperor. The beast is Antichrist. The ten kings give their power to the beast because:

(1) they observe that the beast is raised from death, and thus consider him a superman.

(2) they are enticed by the evil spirit. The Holy Spirit descends from heaven after the death and resurrection of Christ and so the church is formed. Now as a counterfeit, the evil spirit—after the appearing of Antichrist through some kind of resurrection—moves the ten kings to yield their power to the beast.

17.14 According to the order of narration 17.14 precedes 17.16; but according to the order of fact the event of 17.16 happens before that of 17.14. In 19.11–21 we have a detailed description of the war mentioned in 17.14, for the war is actually fought at that time. Though many there will be of those who follow the Lamb, the victory is gained by the Lamb himself. By the sharp sword which proceeds from

His mouth the Lamb shall overcome His enemies and tread them under His feet. He overcomes His enemies, not by power but by authority. He overcomes because He is the King of kings and Lord of lords. This is authority, not power.

Those who accompany the Lamb are marked as having three qualifications—(1) called, (2) chosen, and (3) faithful. They stand in contrast to the great harvest. To follow the Lamb, these must be called. God calls us according to His own determinate will. To be chosen usually precedes a being called, but here it is mentioned after the matter of being called. Hence it refers to a being chosen from among the believers ("Many are called, but few chosen," says the Lord—Matt. 22.14). Such therefore is the order. Psalm 89.19f. may be used to illustrate the meaning here. The children of Israel have already been chosen by God, yet David is further chosen out of the children of Israel. All who are called are saved, but only those who are after God's own heart are the overcomers. Those who are saved form one class, and those who overcome form another class. Whoever follows the Lamb needs to be not only called and chosen but also faithful, which means being mindful of the Lord alone and nothing of self.

17.15 This verse explains the significance of the waters. Since the harlot is a mystery, and therefore symbolic in meaning and not to be interpreted literally, so the waters too must be "mysterious", symbolic, and not subject to literal interpretation. Were we to have Christ as our full satisfaction we would never sit upon many waters. To broaden the fellowship of the saints by having open intercourse with the world is to sit upon many waters.

This woman in the book of Revelation sits on three places:

(1) upon the beast (17.3), which is to say, she is united with Rome;

(2) upon seven mountains (17.9), which means she makes Rome her center; and

(3) upon many waters (17.15), indicating that her influence extends to the entire world.

Why is she sometimes called "harlot" and sometimes "woman"? The term woman is used in relation to Rome, and the term harlot, in relation to Christ—woman, politically speaking; but harlot, religiously speaking.

17.16 The ten horns and the beast hate the harlot, not the woman. For the woman (the city of Rome, cf. 17.18) is their kingdom. They hate the harlot because she is at least in name linked with Christ.

The beast in this book points both to Rome and to Antichrist. We have already learned that Antichrist will be Nero resurrected. Now if he fiercely persecuted Christians once before, would he ever permit Rome to belong to Christ upon his coming back? The first act he performs, therefore, will be the destroying of the harlot.

The reasons for the hatred of the world as personified by Nero are as follows:

(1) On the one hand, because the conduct of the harlot is either too presumptuous or too wicked. Though their conscience is not enlightened by God, the nations of the world cannot tolerate the practices of the Roman Church, such as, that after the bread is blessed by the priest it somehow is transsubstantiated into the body of the Lord, that only the priests can read the Bible, that confession must be made to the priests, and that the inquisition and the selling of indulgences flourish. Yet there are many other mean and treacherous acts practiced by her which even the nations cannot stand.

(2) On the other hand, because of her good, since in the Roman Church there can yet be found such truths taught as the Trinity, Jesus the Son of God, the Virgin Birth, the belief in the Lord's death, resurrection and ascension, and so forth. She still belongs to Christ in name, and therefore the nations hate her.

The ways the world shall treat the Roman Church are:

(1) make her desolate—probably the Vatican where the pope resides will become a desolate place;

(2) make her naked—which, taken literally, may mean the loss of material things, or taken spiritually, may mean the disclosure of her secrets;

(3) eat her flesh—which, spiritually applied, perhaps means the slaying of her great men or the killing of Roman Catholics in general; and

(4) burn her utterly with fire—There is no difficulty in this being taken literally.

The kings of the earth, however, are the Roman Church's bosom friends. Yet, when they see her calamity they only bemoan her but do not help her (18.9,10). Though the seventh king is also her friend, he will nonetheless be there only temporarily (17.10), so neither is he of any help. Antichrist becomes her great enemy.

17.17 The event in this verse probably happens after the great harlot is destroyed. At that time it would appear that the kingdom of Antichrist has come.

17.18 The woman here speaks of Rome, since in John's time only Rome was the great city which reigned over the kings of the earth.

18.1 The person mentioned here must be Christ himself. Besides Him, who ever can have such great authority and who else can lighten the earth with his glory?

18.2 God has destroyed religious Rome through the beast and ten horns (17.16). Now He himself will come to destroy the city of Rome. Hence, this mighty proclamation. This event is also foretold in the Old Testament. In Isaiah 13.21 we read this: "And wild goats shall dance there" (the Septuagint renders it as: "and demons shall dance there"). Though the scene in Isaiah 34.13–15 refers directly to Edom, it is nevertheless quite similar to what is announced here in 18.2.

18.3 This verse speaks of three things:
(1) the nations ("By the wine of the wrath of her fornication all the nations are fallen"). See also 17.2, which, because of what we have said earlier, indicates that religious Rome is in view.
(2) The kings of the earth (they "committed fornication with her"). See 17.2 and 18.9, which in view of what has been said previously, show that both religious and political Rome are involved.
(3) The merchants of the earth (they "waxed rich by the power of her wantonness"). See 18.15, which points specifically to the commercial aspect of Rome.
By reading and considering the last clause of 18.3 we may see God's view on commerce. There will not be any trading in the new heaven and the new earth. Trade prospers here because of luxury. Here commerce is a catering to personal gain as well as to men's luxury. It apparently is not a commendable activity in the sight of God.

18.4 "Her" means the city of Rome as well as religious Rome. According to prophetic history, after the seven bowls have been poured out there follow lightnings and voices and thunders and an earthquake (16.17,18). Then, God remembers the great city of Babylon and He also then sends great hail to the earth (16.19,21). Chapter 17 tells us that Babylon is that great harlot, for upon her forehead is written Mystery, Babylon the Great. It also shows us her past history, the appearing of Antichrist, and her end (vv.1–8). Chapter 18 again informs us how Babylon will fall.

"Come forth, my people, out of her"—This is a command. Although it is given at this juncture, it certainly is applicable to those in view in chapter 17 as well, because there are true believers in the Lord even in religious Rome.

18.5 This verse agrees with 16.19. Both passages speak of how the entire great Babylon is destroyed by God.

As soon as God remembers a sin, He immediately punishes. When He remembers, He remembers clearly; and when He forgets, He also forgets clearly.

18.6 This fulfills the words in Romans 2.6–9. "Render unto her even as she rendered, and double unto her the double according to her works"—Will not the "double" conflict with "according to her works"? Possibly this is due to the dual aspects of Babylon.

"The cup which she mingled"—When in the future God shall arise to judge the city of Rome, He will also judge it for the sins of religious Rome.

18.7 The church does not glorify herself, instead she glorifies Christ. But Rome acts oppositely. She not only glorifies herself but indulges herself luxuriously.

18.8 Mourning comes after sorrow. God judges "the

great city" (18.10) with sorrows, and causes her to mourn. "Lord God" is God's name in the Old Testament, thus indicating that He has returned to His Old Testament position.

18.9 The kings of the earth have no strength to help the woman. For this judgment upon her is an act done by God; therefore, it is beyond their capability. The harlot mentioned in 17.16 is burned, and so too is this city burned.

18.10 "Woe, woe," lament the kings of the earth. In this chapter, this exclamation is recorded as occurring three times—in verses 10, 16 and 19.

18.11 Many maintain that according to its geographical location, Rome cannot become a center of trade. But please notice that 18.11 does not say that this city is the center of import and export. For besides what Rome has bought, there is nothing else in it to sell. Rome buys profusely because Antichrist lives there in great luxury.

18.12-13 There are seven different kinds of commodities mentioned: (1) jewelry, (2) fabrics, (3) vessels, (4) perfumes, (5) delicacies, (6) herds, flocks, horses and chariots, and (7) slaves and souls of men. The last commodity, "slaves and souls", may also be translated bodies and souls. A popular saying of the period goes like this: "What Babylon keeps is first gold and last of all souls."

18.14 This verse speaks of Rome's past.

18.15,16 This time it is the merchants who cry "Woe, woe" (v.16). Compare 18.16 with 17.4 and it can be seen that they fit each other exactly.

18.17 "For in one hour . . . is made desolate"—This sentence is connected with the preceding verse.

18.17–19 This time it is the shipmasters and the mariners who cry "Woe, woe" (v.19).
"In one hour" are words spoken three times in this book of Revelation: (1) by the kings of the earth (18.10), (2) by the merchants (18.17), and (3) by the shipmasters, the mariners, and the passengers (18.19).

18.20 The saints and the prophets probably include both the Old and the New Testament saints and prophets.

18.21 We do not know how God will destroy Babylon. We only know that God remembers the Great Babylon just at the time of the great earthquake (16.19). So perhaps Babylon is destroyed by an earthquake. Usually there is fire after an earthquake. This is why the kings of the earth, the merchants, and others look upon the smoke of her burning but are hindered from going in to rescue her (18.9,10).

18.22,23 Altogether, the words "no more at all" appear six times in verses 21–23.

18.22–24 These verses disclose three reasons (they are actually sins) to explain why God judges Babylon:
(1) "Thy merchants were the princes of the earth";
(2) "With thy sorcery were all the nations deceived"; and
(3) "In her was found the blood of prophets and of saints, and of all that have been slain upon the earth."
The fault with modern commerce is not in balancing needs with supplies but in ensnaring people; therefore, it is

apparently sinful. Sorcery is a holding intercourse with demons. It could be that Rome will become the center of sorcery in the future. Rome, of course, has shed—and will yet shed—lots of human blood.

19.1-6 The events covered by this section follow upon those which 18.24 concludes.

19.1 "After these things"—that is, after Babylon is completely destroyed. "A great multitude"—this includes all those who are saved (not just those saved during the age of grace). "Hallelujah" is literally "Alleluia", which means "Praise the Lord" in Greek. Why Alleluia? Because salvation and glory and power have now come.

19.2 The sentence "True and righteous are his judgments" coincides with "Righteous and true are thy ways" found in 15.3. True because God judges according to actual conditions; righteous because God judges in accordance with proper procedures. The judgment of the great harlot (religious Rome) is quoted to prove that God is righteous.

19.3 The judgment of Rome will last forever and ever.

19.4 This is the last time in the Bible when the 24 elders and the four living creatures are mentioned. After the great multitude in heaven says "Hallelujah", the 24 elders and the four living creatures respond with "Amen, Hallelujah"—indicating thereby that the latter group is different from the former group. The great multitude in heaven speak of salvation, glory, power, and so forth; thus showing plainly that the church is included. The 24 elders do not represent the church. Hereafter they will no longer be mentioned, since after this time they must have resigned from their lofty positions.

19.5 This is the last time that the throne is mentioned as being in the temple, because at the present moment there is a temple but not a city. In the new heaven and the new earth there will only be the city but not a temple.

"Voice . . . from the throne" must be referring to the voice of the Lord Jesus because the Lamb is "in the midst of the throne" (5.6).

"All ye his servants" is a phrase pointing to those in the church, since this book emphasizes the individual responsibility of believers before God.

"Ye that fear him" are words that refer to all who fear God, both of the Jews and of the Gentiles.

"Give praise to our God"—This is what the Lord always does (Heb. 2.12).

19.6 "Voice of a great multitude"—it being the voice of a great many people. "Voice of many waters"—this being the resounding voice of the great multitude. "Voice of mighty thunders"—it being the sound of majesty and grandeur.

"For the Lord our God, the Almighty, reigneth"—The Almighty has always reigned, only now this fact is being manifested.

19.7 Who is this "wife" of the Lamb? It cannot be the church for the following reasons:

(1) The great multitude spoken of in 19.1 includes the saved among the children of Israel as well as from among the nations. The church is definitely included. Since it is the

great multitude who proclaims the words found in 19.7, the church must therefore be included among those who make such a proclamation. And hence the wife must point to someone else.

(2) In the parable of the ten virgins (Matt. 25.1–13), only the five wise virgins (and therefore not all who are in the church, for notice that all ten *are* virgins) are privileged to attend the marriage feast.

(3) This wife of the Lamb is different from the bride in Paul's epistles. For she whom Paul speaks of is clothed with Christ, whereas the wife here is clothed with her own righteousnesses. In Paul's epistles the church as a whole is viewed as the bride of Christ. In Revelation, the church is considered according to her components, therefore the responsibility of the church before God is stressed. In Paul's epistles the church is accepted in Christ, but in Revelation the church is accepted in her works. In Paul's epistles the church in totality belongs to Christ, while in Revelation she is divided into the saved and the overcomers.

This wife of the Lamb is none other than the New Jerusalem (21.9,10).

God is now in His holy temple, so that the voices of praise from the great multitude come also from the temple. During the millennial kingdom the overcomers shall be kings in the city and priests in the temple. But the temple shall gradually lose its prominence until it totally disappears, for God and the Lamb will be the temple in New Jerusalem in the new heaven and the new earth.

Of the church, some (for example, the five wise virgins) will attend the marriage feast, while some (for example, the five foolish virgins) will not be able to attend the marriage feast.

19.8 The wife of the Lamb, as we have seen from the

above discussion, signifies the New Jerusalem. "It was given to her" are words to indicate reward. "Bright" is due to the whiteness of the fine linen. This is in direct contrast to the clothing of the great harlot (17.4). "Pure" here is in perfect agreement with the word "pure" in 19.14.

"For the fine linen is the righteousnesses of the saints" (Darby)—The word "righteousnesses" is the same as is found in Isaiah 64: "our righteousnesses" (v.6).

These saints will soon be inhabitants of the city of New Jerusalem. The duration of time as a bride is limited, but as a wife it is from start to finish. So, too, is this the case with New Jerusalem. During the millennial kingdom, New Jerusalem is the bride of the Lamb. And in the new heaven and new earth New Jerusalem will be the wife of the Lamb.

Christians are divided into the saved and the overcomers. Only the overcoming believers are related to the new city during the millennial kingdom. In the new heaven and new earth, both the saved and the overcomers partake equally in New Jerusalem.

The wedding gown is worn only for a time; the believers who overcome are joined together as the bride.

At the marriage of the Lamb it looks as though the door of New Jerusalem is opened for the first time to let in the overcomers. The five foolish virgins are not able to enter at this time.

19.9 This verse shows us explicitly that some people are invited, and blessed are those who *are* invited to the marriage. This city is the bride of the Lamb, and those who enjoy the glory and the beauty of the city are the invited ones who have the righteousnesses of the saints. (It is also true that these righteousnesses constitute the very glory and beauty of the city.)

"These are true words of God"—This is repeated twice

more in 21.5 and 22.6. It is used to call our special attention to what has just been said. Some may regard the invitation to the marriage of the Lamb as insignificant, though as a matter of fact only those who are so invited have any share in the kingdom. All who are not invited to the marriage have no part in the kingdom. Only the believers who overcome are entitled to participate in the marriage feast. This seems to agree with Revelation 3.20 wherein the thought of supping with the Lord is also present.

19.10 Angels are servants of God. It is a great temptation to us to worship created beings.

"The spirit of prophecy" is related to "the spirits of the prophets" (1 Cor. 14.32), since it is the prophet who prophesies.

19.11 The marriage ceremony being over, now the Lord comes down to the earth with His faithful followers. These names "Faithful and True" have already been spoken of in chapter 1 of this book. Here they are the names of our Lord in His second coming, and they reveal His relationship to the world; in chapter 1, however, these names are especially connected with the church.

19.12 "Diadems" are crowns. They can be worn layer upon layer because they have no tops. The "name" mentioned here is so special that no one knows but He himself. In 2.17 it is recorded that the Lord promises to give to the overcomers in the church at Pergamum a new name which no one knows but they who have received it. Therefore, this special name of the Lord is also given to Him by God.

19.13 "And he is arrayed in a garment sprinkled

with blood"—The garment is not sprinkled with blood in heaven, rather it is so sprinkled in the battle on earth. This describes the scene of the battle of Har-Magedon (see also Is. 13.1–6).

"The Word of God"—Only John had used such an expression before (John 1.1), thus proving that John wrote this book.

19.14 Those here who follow the Lamb ("the armies which are in heaven") are the same as the called and chosen and faithful mentioned in 17.14. By this time the standings of the Christians have already been determined. All who are invited to the marriage feast of the Lamb may enter the kingdom because:

(1) The garment of the bride is the righteousnesses of the saints.

(2) The righteousnesses of the saints, in turn, are the glory and beauty of the new city.

(3) All who are invited to the marriage feast of the Lamb must possess the righteousnesses of the saints. Those who come with the Lord are those who have been invited to the marriage feast of the Lamb. Hence all who enter the kingdom have been invited to the marriage feast of the Lamb.

(4) As recorded in Mark, the Lord used these words: "Until that day when I drink it new in the kingdom of God" (14.25). This indicates that the feast is to be enjoyed in the kingdom.

(5) The "sup with him, and he with me" of Revelation 3.20 agrees with the words "Blessed are they that are bidden to the marriage supper of the Lamb" of 19.9.

(6) The "blessed" in 19.9 is related to the "blessed" in 20.6.

(7) In the kingdom, the New Jerusalem is the bride; in

the new heaven and the new earth, New Jerusalem is the wife of the Lamb. Yet even then, at the time of 21.9, she still retains the form of a bride.

19.15 This verse declares three things concerning the Lord:

(1) "Out of his mouth proceedeth a sharp sword"—This is the word that comes out of His mouth.

(2) "A rod of iron"—Three times is this mentioned in the book, the other two places being 2.27 and 12.5. At the commencement of the kingdom He will break all powers of resistance.

(3) "Treadeth the winepress of the fierceness of the wrath of God"—This is in agreement with 14.17–20 and Isaiah 13.1–6.

19.16 His thigh is especially mentioned because He rides on a horse.

19.17,18 "The marriage supper of the Lamb" spoken of in 19.9 is for those who are invited; "the great supper of God" here is for "all the birds that fly in mid heaven" (v.17).

19.19,20 These verses tell of the destinies of the beast and the false prophet. Observe the following sequence of events:

(1) 19.11–16 relates how the Lord fights and wins the battle.

(2) 19.17–18 rehearses how the birds eat the flesh of the defeated.

(3) 19.19–20 tells the end of the beast and of the false prophet.

The false prophet has done three things. He has:

(1) "wrought the signs in his [the beast's] sight";

(2) "Deceived them that had received the mark of the beast"; and

(3) "Deceived . . . them that worshipped his [the beast's] image . . ."

"Alive into"—Please notice this word. It coincides with our explanations of 13.11 and 13.18. For both beast and false prophet come back from death; and since their flesh cannot die twice, they are cast alive into the lake of fire.

19.21 After the events which this verse concludes, then those Christians who faithfully have followed the Lord shall enjoy glory a thousand years ahead of other Christians.

20.1-3 SATAN IS BOUND

20.1,2 It is said in 9.1 that the key to the pit of the abyss is given to Satan, with which he there and then does two things:

(1) He causes two persons to return to life.

(2) He releases the beasts out of the pit to hurt men.

Satan is cast out of heaven after the war in heaven (12.7–9). Now he is cast into the abyss (20.3), for the Lord is the King of kings and the Lord of lords (19.16 and 20.1). The Lord overcomes Satan by authority, and His word is full of authority.

20.3 Some may ask why the dragon is not immediately thrown into the lake of fire. The answer is that after he has been shut in for a thousand years, the dragon is to be released temporarily for the following reasons:

(1) to prove that the dragon will never repent,

(2) to unveil the hidden sins of men, and
(3) to show the good pleasure of God.

20.4 Three classes of people will reign with Christ:

(1) The overcomers will sit on thrones, and judgment will be given to them (20.4a). This shows that they have inherited the kingdom (see also Dan. 7.10,18,22—"Saints of the Most High").

(2) The martyrs throughout the 20 centuries ("them that had been beheaded"—20.4b). These are the souls under the altar as shown in the fifth seal (6.9f.). It is for "the testimony of Jesus" that they are killed.

(3) The martyrs during the Great Tribulation. These are those who do not worship the beast nor his image, and upon whose foreheads and hands no mark of the beast is received (20.4c).

"They lived"—Let us notice two things:

(1) These people are not resurrected at the time of 20.4. Their resurrection is merely retraced here as an accomplished fact. John does not see them resurrected at that moment; he only acknowledges that they live.

(2) Those here who live include not only the resurrected but also those who are raptured alive; for we cannot assert that only those who are resurrected reign here with Christ; since even though the number of people who are raptured alive may not be great they nevertheless shall reign with Christ too.

20.5 "The first resurrection"—This does not necessarily mean that there is only one resurrection, nor does it denote that there are many resurrections. It simply signifies this as being the "best" resurrection.

The word "the" includes the two things mentioned in the last clause of 20.4:

(1) "Lived" and (2) "reigned": The best resurrection means to live and to reign. Such a resurrection is a reward, for there is a reigning with Christ for a thousand years as well as a being resurrected.

"The second death" of 20.6 is in contrast with "the first resurrection", because the latter means to enjoy glory while the former means to suffer eternally. Hence the first resurrection is none other than the time of recompense (Luke 14.14, 20.34–36).

What Paul says in Philippians 3.11 is not an expecting to be raised from the dead (for all the dead shall be resurrected), nor an anticipating the resurrection of the spirit (for the resurrection of the spirit is already accomplished at the time of new birth). No, what Paul is looking forward to is the "out-resurrection" from among the dead, which is this "best" resurrection spoken of here in 20.5, even a reigning with the Lord.

Read again Philippians 1.23–25. There in that epistle's first chapter Paul is saying that he will live; he is not contemplating death. How, then, can he be talking about resurrection? He clearly states in Philippians 3.20,21 that he waits for the coming of the Lord. Consequently, what he anxiously hopes for is to reign with the Lord.

"The rest of the dead" naturally includes all the unsaved sinners. Their resurrection will come to pass a thousand years later.

20.6 "Blessed" should be translated literally as "happy"—Those who appear to be happy today may not be holy, while those who are holy can hardly be happy today.

The first resurrection is blessed in three ways:

(1) "Over these the second death hath no power"—The

second death is the lake of fire. Those who have no part in the first resurrection may yet be hurt by the second death. Some Christians will be disciplined in the future (see Matt. 18.34,35). He who wrongs his brother will be punished by the Lord (1 Thess. 4.5,6). We believers are exhorted to fear Him who has authority to cast into hell (Greek, *gehenna*), thus implying that over some Christians hell still has its threat (Luke 12.4,5). If a branch does not abide in Christ, he, like a branch, is liable to be cast off, withered, cast into the fire and burned (John 15.6).

Some, though, may ask, Does not the Bible teach that once a person is saved he will never perish? Why then do you say here that Christians may appear as though to perish? This is due none other than to a misunderstanding of some Scripture verses such as the following:

"He shall never see death" (John 8.51,52) is actually "he shall not forever see death" in the original, and "he shall never taste of death" is "he shall not forever taste death" in the original.

"They shall never perish" (John 10.28) is "they shall not forever perish" in the original.

"Shall never die" (John 11.25,26) is "shall not forever die" in the original.

(2) "They shall be priests of God and of Christ"—The significance of a priest is to draw near to God. This people shall be very close to God for they shall have a special relationship with Him and Christ. Today we all are priests, therefore all may draw nigh to God. But in the millennial kingdom only those who have part in the first resurrection shall function as priests to God and to Christ.

Aaron functioned as priest because his rod budded. The budded rod represents resurrection. Whoever is chosen priest is proven by resurrection.

When the children of Israel came out of Egypt they all

were destined to be priests (Ex.19.6). Due to their worshiping the golden calf, however, God later chose the family
of Aaron to be priests.

"They shall be priests . . . of Christ", since at this time
Christ shall receive worship as much as God himself is
worshiped.

(3) "And shall reign with him a thousand years"—As a
rule, in Old Testament times no king was able to be a
priest, and no priest, a king. But here is a people who are
both priests and kings. As priests, they draw near to God; as
kings, they rule over the earth. Only those who have
suffered are entitled to reign and enjoy glory with Christ.

Here we are told only the fact that they do reign, we are
not informed as to *how* they reign. No doubt the reigning
here is heavenly in nature.

PART TEN

AFTER THE MILLENNIUM

After the Millennium
(20.7–22.5)

20.7,8 Generally speaking the Old Testament prophets foresaw things up to the time of the millennium. They are not very clear on matters that are to occur after the millennium. What is mentioned in the section before us here, however, are events which are to happen after the millennium.

Some may raise the question of how people in the millennial kingdom could be deceived after the thousand years are passed. We should be aware that during the millennium there are two classes of people on earth:

(1) The Jews—They "shall be all righteous" (Is. 60.21).

(2) The good nations (Matt. 25.34–40,46)—The bad nations have been slain (Rev. 19.21); the sheep nations shall inherit the kingdom.

Although during the millennium there are these two classes of people, the Jews hold a much higher position than do the nations.

These people in the millennium are human beings with flesh and blood, and they still beget sons and daughters. The first generation of the nations may be saved, but the children they beget may not be saved. Isaiah 65.20 mentions death, thus indicating that sin still exists even at this time.

Zechariah 14.17 speaks of people who will still refuse to

worship the Lord. The Lord and His Christians shall rule the nations with an iron rod, that is to say, they shall use force to subjugate people. Whoever disobeys shall be instantly broken. Whoever acts evilly shall immediately be destroyed. Satan can easily deceive this group of people when he is temporarily released.

"Magog" is mentioned in Genesis 10.2. "Gog" is seen in Numbers 24.7 where "Agag" is translated "Gog" in the Septuagint. According to the writings of the Arabs, Magog and Gog occupied the vast expanse of Russia, Mongolia, and even to the eastern border of Germany. They were nomads and were very fierce. Some call the Mongolians the Tartars. Their ancestors hated the Jews very much.

20.9 "The breadth of the earth"—the "earth" here speaks of the Jewish land. The rebellious crowds come in such number that they shall spread over all the Jewish territory.

"The camp of the saints" is where the Christians live. Being "the armies which are in heaven" (19.14), they only encamp temporarily on earth. Encampment is something transient, for the millennial kingdom too will pass away.

"The beloved city" is the city where the Jews live. Being in such high position, they are to be envied and therefore attacked.

20.10   THE ETERNAL END OF SATAN

The counterfeit trinity is now in the lake of fire.

Some may question why there is still day and night. Shortly we shall see that the Bible merely states that "the city hath no need of the sun, neither of the moon, to shine upon it" (Rev. 21.23). It does not say that there is no need of the sun and the moon in the new heaven and the new earth. Even the tree of life shall bear fruits each month. If there is neither sun nor moon, how can there be monthly fruit-bearing?

20.11-15 "THE JUDGMENT OF THE GREAT WHITE THRONE"

20.11 This throne is different from the one in chapters 4 and 5. The description of the throne here is modified by two adjectives:

(1) "Great"—for this judgment is most extraordinary. It is great in righteousness.

(2) "White"—which color has special relation to the Lord; for example, the Lord's hair is white and He rides on a white horse. White signifies being perfectly pure and absolutely righteous.

"Him that sat upon it"—No doubt He is the Lord. We have many proofs in the New Testament about this; for instance, John 5.22, Acts 10.42 and 17.31, Romans 2.6, 1 Peter 4.5, and 2 Timothy 4.1.

"The earth and the heaven fled away"—Some consider this fleeing of the earth and heaven as only a divine act of re-making, but the succeeding clause, "and there was found no place for them", clearly shows that the old heaven and earth are completely destroyed; for there is the mark of sin in the old creation. This fulfills what is prophesied in 2 Peter 3.4,10,12. Evidently God sends fire with which to burn up the old heaven and earth.

20.12 "The dead" are "the rest of the dead" spoken of in 20.5. The phrase "standing before the throne" demonstrates that they are living, therefore they must be resurrected.

Will there be anyone saved at the Great White Throne? The answer is yes for the following reasons:

(1) This is a judgment. Judgment is a matter of determining as well as sentencing. If all are perished people, a mere proclamation of condemnation would be sufficient. Why should they be judged at all?

(2) Here are opened not only the books which record the works of everyone but also the book of life in which all the names of the saved are inscribed. May not all this suggest that some names are in the books of works while some are in the book of life?

(3) The Lord Jesus explicitly states that at the last day of resurrection some shall be saved: "For the hour cometh . . . they that have done good, unto the resurrection of life; and they that have done evil, unto the resurrection of judgment" (John 5.28,29).

(4) Facing fact, it seems hardly possible that there would be no saved people at the judgment, for the reasons listed below:

(a) There will be people who die during the millennial kingdom. If they are resurrected at this moment, can it be that there are no saved souls among them?

(b) Many will have lived before the kingdom comes. They have no part in the first resurrection. If they appear at this time, will there not be saved souls?

(c) The spirits of those believers who have been excommunicated or who have remained unrepentant shall be saved in the day of the Lord Jesus. If they should appear at this hour, how can they not be saved?

(d) The Bible explicitly states that those who do not confess Christ before men will not be confessed by Christ before the angels of God. This means they have no part in the kingdom. If they too were to appear at this juncture, they certainly should be among the saved.

(e) During the Old Testament period many were

saved though unfit to reign with Christ. Were they to appear at this moment, they no doubt would be among the saved.

(f) Many have died in infancy. If they are not saved then, when will they be saved?

(5) Besides the resurrected dead there are the living Israelites (as a matter of fact, the whole nation of Israel) who shall stand before the throne; can we say that they are not saved? Moreover, there are the nations that do not follow Satan at the last rebellion; again, can we say that they are not saved?

"Books" is plural in number. "According to their works" means (1) the judgment is based on works, and (2) punishment is measured out according to the quality of their works.

20.13 "Death and Hades gave up the dead that were in them"—This is a matter of delivering up the souls of men that they may be judged.

"And the sea gave up the dead that were in it"—possibly because the abyss and the sea are closely linked; and in the abyss are imprisoned the spirits.

"And they were judged every man according to their works"—This is mentioned twice (vv. 12 and 13) because the future judgment is entirely based on works.

20.14 Death is the last enemy to be destroyed (1 Cor. 15.25–26, 55–56).

20.15 To put this verse positively, if anyone's name is found written in the book of life, that one is definitely saved.

Hence the judgment of the Great White Throne is according to principles: Those who perish perish because of their evil works (not because of their good works), and those who are saved are saved because their names are written in the book of life (not because of their good works).

21.1–8 "A NEW HEAVEN AND A NEW EARTH"

Special attention should be given to the sub-divisions that follow.

a. 21.1 The Throne of the New Heaven and the New Earth

The old heaven and the old earth are passed away; now is there the new heaven and the new earth. There is no mentioning of a new sea. In Isaiah 65.17 God is recorded as declaring that He will create a new heaven and a new earth, but what follows after verse 17 actually refers to the millennial kingdom. The outline of Isaiah 65 is a contrasting of the blessed of God with other people. Verse 17 of Isaiah 65 is a declaration by which God declares that He will create a new heaven and a new earth. Verses 18–25 describe the conditions of Jerusalem in the millennial kingdom.

The new heaven and the new earth which are spoken of in 2 Peter 3.10,13 are the same as those mentioned here in 21.1.

b. 21.2–4 The Relation of New Jerusalem to the People

21.2 This is a holy city. Whereas in the past God had only a holy temple and not a holy city, nevertheless, on the earth and in that holy temple He did dwell; now, though, the holy city supplants the holy temple, and all its inhabitants are priests. The old Jerusalem was built by men and had become old; the New Jerusalem comes down from

heaven and is wholly new. During the millennial kingdom
the New Jerusalem is suspended in the air. It has not
descended to the earth because on earth there is yet the old
Jerusalem. When the New Jerusalem does come down from
heaven it seems from the record here that she has not yet
taken off her bridal attire. At the time of the marriage
supper of the Lamb she is the bride. Now in eternity she is
to be the wife of the Lamb.

21.3 "A great voice"—It might be the voice of the
Lord Jesus.

"He shall dwell with them"—Hereafter there is no
longer any distinction between Jews and Gentiles. Those
whom God calls are just men.

"The tabernacle of God is with men"—The New
Jerusalem is on earth like God's tabernacle. Formerly,
God's tabernacle was set on earth among the children of
Israel; now, there being no more distinction between Jews
and Gentiles, the tabernacle of God is set among men. God
is now with men.

"And they shall be his peoples"—Henceforth they shall
belong to God and shall delight in His word. "And God
himself shall be with them, and be their God"—He shall
watch over them according to His good pleasure, that is to
say, God will be gracious to them (see Jer. 24.7, Ez.
11.18–20).

21.4 "Tear"—Tears are the common lot of men on
earth. But now, God shall wipe away their tears by
eliminating their causes such as death, mourning, pain, and
so forth. All these are the results of sin. When these are
ruled out, there remains no longer any trace of sin.

c. 21.5–8 The Difference between the Saved and Those Who Perish

Even though this subdivision is closely related to the preceding one (vv.2–4), the people in verse 6b are nonetheless quite different from those in verse 3.

21.5 The one who sits on the throne is most likely God.

The word "write" means to have it written in this book. Such a command reveals the great significance of this subdivision.

21.6 "They are come to pass"—Whatever is recorded in this book must come to pass. God will bring heaven and earth to His original design. He is the Alpha and the Omega, therefore all shall be fulfilled.

21.7 The "overcometh" here is not the same as that of chapters 2 and 3, for in chapters 2 and 3 it is an overcoming by works, that is, an overcoming that involves a comparing of believers with believers; whereas here it is an overcoming that involves a comparison of believers with the unbelieving world (cf. 1 John 5.4 which mentions overcoming the world through faith).

In what respects are the people spoken of in 21.6–8 different from the people who appear in verses 2 and 3? Please note the following observations.

(1) From 21.3 we learn that John saw in a vision that the tabernacle of God is with men, that is to say, God is dwelling with the many peoples on earth. The people mentioned in 21.6b are said to be those who are athirst after they have heard the good news described above.

(2) The men shown in verses 2 and 3 are God's peoples

who dwell on the new earth, while those shown in 21.7 are God's sons who live in the city.

(3) The men mentioned in 21.3 are simply those peoples on earth who share together the common blessings; but the men referred to in 21.7 are not only sons of God, they are also God's servants and kings unto Him (22.3,5).

(4) "They shall be his peoples" (21.3) signifies something corporate and common; "He shall be my son" (21.7) represents something personal and intimate.

(5) "They shall be his peoples" (21.3) is that which appears to be spoken in the third person, whereas "I will be his God, and he shall be my son" (21.7) seems to be a direct way of speaking.

(6) The men spoken of in 21.3 dwell on God's earth, but those mentioned in 21.7 live in God's house.

Positional difference among Christians is limited to the time of the millennial kingdom. In the new heaven and new earth, all believers are equally positioned.

21.8 "The fearful"—these are those who know they can be saved if they believe, yet dare not believe for fear of men. "Unbelieving"—these are those who just do not believe. "Abominable"—a reference to not only those who worship idols but also to those who worship celestial bodies. "Sorcerers"—those who have communications with demons.

"The lake that burneth with fire and brimstone"—In the new heaven and new earth there is no sea, yet there will still be the lake of fire.

21.9-27 "THE NEW JERUSALEM"

21.9 Now the name of the wife of the Lamb is given. Many people consider the church to be the wife of the

Lamb since, they say, there cannot be a literal New Jerusalem in the future. Many are the proofs, however, that the New Jerusalem is a literal new city:

(1) At that time the church as we know it today no longer exists, for she now becomes only a part of all the redeemed.

(2) Being a book of revelation, its chapters 2 and 3 plainly point out the churches quite clearly and specifically; why then should the New Jerusalem mentioned in chapter 21 of this same book be something other than the clearly stated and specifically mentioned New Jerusalem?

(3) According to 3.12 the New Jerusalem is what the church hopes for. If New Jerusalem is indeed the church, how could the church hope for the church? It would be senseless and illogical.

(4) In 19.7–13 the New Jerusalem is seen as the bride whereas the church is a guest, thus showing that the church is not New Jerusalem.

(5) How can there be no new city in the new heaven and the new earth? Where will people stay if they come to worship God? Did not our Lord expressly say that "in my Father's house are many mansions" (John 14.2)?

(6) If the woman mentioned in 12.1 refers to Jerusalem and the great harlot cited in 17.1 points to the city of Rome, how can the wife of the Lamb spoken of in 21.9 not be a reference to an actual city?

(7) After the blowing of the seventh trumpet the kingdom has arrived and the mystery is fulfilled. Since New Jerusalem subsists in the new heaven and the new earth, it cannot be considered a mystery, and therefore it must be literal.

(8) At the time of chapter 17 when John sees Babylon, he cannot cease wondering because it is a mystery which must be explained by an angel to him. Here, though, John

is not amazed at all, neither does he need an angel to interpret to him. Hence what is here before us must be an actual city.

(9) People deem the wife of the Lamb to be the church because they adopt a totally spiritual view of eternity. Who knows, though, but what in the new heaven and the new earth everything is real and substantial? If God chose to use gold and silver in the building of Solomon's temple, why can there not be gold and silver in the building by God of a new city in the new heaven and the new earth?

(10) Since many at that time are to be resurrected bodily, that is, they are to have a spiritual *body*, will they not need a place to stay?

(11) Here we are told the structure, dimensions, and materials of the city of New Jerusalem. These can hardly be applied to the church.

(12) 21.27 plainly implies that many will enter the city. If the city is the church which is itself made up of people, how can people enter into people? Furthermore, 21.25 says that the gates of the city are not shut by day. How can this fact be something related to the church?

(13) Here in 21.9 the wife of the Lamb is shown to John. Now if the wife of the Lamb is a mystery and the New Jerusalem is an explanation, how can an explanation not be taken literally?

(14) The New Jerusalem is contrasted with the Old Jerusalem. As Old Jerusalem is a literal city, so New Jerusalem must also be a literal city. It therefore cannot be taken as the church.

(15) Galatians 4 distinctly tells us that "the Jerusalem that is above is free, which is our mother" (v.26). This Jerusalem is quite different from the church, so Paul says it is our (that is, the church's) mother. Thus we cannot maintain that New Jerusalem is the church.

(16) Hebrews 11 says that Abraham "looked for the city which hath the foundations, whose builder and maker is God" (v.10). The New Jerusalem is a true city with foundations. Did Abraham look for the church? He could not have known the church at his time.

(17) Hebrews 12.22 mentions the heavenly Jerusalem and the innumerable hosts of angels. Verse 23 of the same chapter speaks of the general assembly and church of the firstborn who are enrolled in heaven (this means the church), speaks also of God who is the Judge of all, and of spirits of just men made perfect (the saints of old). There are altogether five classes enumerated here; namely, (1) God, (2) angels, (3) saints of the Old Testament time, (4) the church, and (5) the heavenly Jerusalem. The church and the heavenly Jerusalem are listed separately, therefore they cannot be the same.

[*Translator's Note:* When Mr. Nee first gave these Bible readings on Revelation in the early days of his ministry he adopted a more literal interpretation of the holy city, New Jerusalem. In his later work, already quoted from earlier in this study and first entitled in Chinese as *Holy and Without Blemish* (but subsequently published in Chinese under the title *The Glorious Church*), the author took a more spiritual approach to its interpretation. What follows below are some highlights from this approach, translated directly from the first Chinese edition of Shanghai, 1953, pp. 133–155.]

21.10 "And he carried me away in the Spirit to a mountain great and high"—If we wish to see the eternal vision of God we need to be brought by God to a great and high mountain. Unless we stand on a spiritual high mountain we cannot see anything. Those who live on the plain will not be able to see the New Jerusalem—the finality of God's work.

"The holy city Jerusalem, coming down out of heaven from God"—The wife of the Lamb whom John saw was the holy city Jerusalem. The description of the city is allegorical. By its description we are told of the corporate body which God from eternity has purposed to obtain.

This is a city which comes out of heaven from God. God pays attention not only to where this corporate man will go but from whence he comes out as well. Not only the destiny but also the source. The wife of the Lamb comes out of heaven, not from earth. God does not show us here the man who has a past history of sin but is now saved by grace. This does not mean of course, that we do not have a history of sin, therefore needing neither repentance nor salvation. This passage of Scripture simply reveals to us that portion which comes out of God, which is the glorious church of Ephesians 5 that is to be presented to Christ.

One characteristic of this new Jerusalem is holiness. Among Christians, some look for greatness, some look for holiness. The former is the principle of Babylon, whereas the latter is the principle of New Jerusalem. What is holiness? We may say that only God is holy; therefore, all that comes out of God is holy: "For both he that sanctifieth and they that are sanctified are all of one" (Heb. 2.11).

21.11 "Having the glory of God . . . a jasper stone"—The God on the throne whom John saw was like a jasper stone (see 4.3). In other words, jasper means the God who is seen. The God whom we know as we stand before His throne is like jasper stone. Our knowledge of God today here on earth is at best termed "darkly" or "in a riddle" (1 Cor. 13.12 mg.); but in the city which has the glory of God like a jasper stone we shall then see Him as He is—"clear as crystal" (v.11).

21.12–14 "Having twelve gates, . . . and names written thereon, which are the names of the twelve tribes of the children of Israel: . . . And the wall of the city had twelve foundations, and on them twelve names of the twelve apostles of the Lamb"—Whom does this corporate man include? Having the twelve names of the tribes of Israel on its gates and the twelve names of the apostles on its foundations, this city includes all the Old and the New Testament saints. At the time of the new heaven and the new earth, all who have the life of God are to be included in the New Jerusalem.

21.15–17 "And he that spake with me had for a measure a golden reed to measure . . . the wall thereof"—Besides the glory of God, the next thing mentioned is the wall of the city. Separation—as depicted here by a wall—is an important principle in Christian living. Lack of separation devaluates the Christian's worth. A line must be drawn between what is spiritual and what is carnal. New Jerusalem has its boundary, its wall of separation. From this we learn that whatever is of Babylon must be rejected and whatever is of God must be protected. Building a city wall is not an easy task; it is greatly hated by Satan. For example, when Nehemiah returned to Jerusalem to build the city wall, he was opposed vehemently by Sanballat and Tobiah. Consequently, with one hand he held his weapon and with the other hand he built. Let us ask God to teach us how to take up spiritual weapons against the spiritual hosts of wickedness in the heavenlies and how at the same time to maintain the principle of separation.

Having the names of the twelve apostles on the foundations means that everything in the city is based on the principle of the kingdom of God as proclaimed by the apostles. "Being built upon the foundation of the apostles and prophets" (Eph. 2.20) simply means that the revelation which the apostles received from the Lord is the foundation of New Jerusalem.

Why are the names of the twelve tribes of Israel written on the doors? The answer is supplied by the words of the Lord Jesus himself, who declared that "salvation is from the Jews" (John 4.22).

The Bible employs gold to represent all that is of God. To measure with a golden reed suggests that this city is measurable by God's standard, for it meets His standard.

"And the city lieth foursquare, . . . the length and the breadth and the height thereof are equal"—In the Scriptures we find that only the holiest of all things in the temple and the New Jerusalem are in perfect cubes. This is thus to imply that in the new heaven and the new earth the New Jerusalem will be the holiest of all to God.

"According to the measure of a man, that is, of an angel"—Why at that time is the measure of a man equal to the measure of an angel? In resurrection, men shall be equal to the angels (Luke 20.36). In other words, all that is in the city is on resurrection ground. That which cannot be bound and retained by death is called resurrection. Whatever comes out of us will be finished at the cross; that which is of God cannot be touched by death.

21.18–21 "And the city was pure gold, like unto pure glass"—One special feature of New Jerusalem is that the gold therein is pure. Everything is wholly of God; there is not a speck of mixture. Whatever is not of God is dross. No one can say to God that he has something in himself to give to Him. What God wants is nothing but pure gold.

"The foundations of the wall of the city were adorned with all manner of precious stones"—There is a basic difference between gold and precious stone. The first is a single chemical element, but the second is a compound. Gold is directly created by God, whereas precious stone is the result of the fusing together of several elements under the earth after they have gone through extremely high temperature accompanied by pressure. In other words, what the precious stone represents is not that which God gives directly to man, rather it stands for the refining work which the Holy Spirit has done in man. The life which God gives to us is gold, the life which God forges in us is precious stone. God does not stop with merely imparting the life of Christ to us; He goes on to incorporate or work into us that life in us.

"And the twelve gates were twelve pearls"—Pearl is formed by the secretion of a mollusk in the sea after it is wounded by a grain of sand or other foreign matter. Hence pearl signifies that life which comes out of death. It represents the life which the Lord Jesus Christ has released in His death on the non-atoning side.

"And the street of the city was pure gold, as it were transparent glass"—A street is a place for fellowship. Inasmuch as the street of the city is pure gold, all who walk on it will never have their feet defiled. Today all who are bathed still need to wash their feet continually (John 13.10) in order to maintain their fellowship with God. For as long as we walk on this earth we cannot help but be contaminated by the dust of the earth, thus affecting our fellowship with God. But the day shall come when nothing will defile us nor hinder our fellowship with God. In eternity nothing defiles us, therefore our whole life shall be holy.

"As it were transparent glass"—Today many situations are opaque, but in the future everything shall be transparent before God. If that is the case, then we must begin to learn even today to be true and transparent, not attempting to pretend to be what we are not.

[Here ends the translated portion of highlights of the author's spiritual approach to an interpretation of the holy city, New Jerusalem, taken directly from Mr. Nee's *Holy and Without Blemish* (Shanghai, 1953, pp. 133–155).—*Translator*]

21.10 "And he carried me away in the Spirit to a mountain great and high"—This is in contrast to the words "And he carried me away in the Spirit into a wilderness" found in 17.3.

21.11 This city especially has the glory of God. Formerly, in the old temple, the glory of God was not too obvious since it appeared like a cloud.

"Her light was like unto a stone most precious, as it were a jasper stone, clear as crystal"—Crystal is transparent. Today even the light of the sun is opaque, but the light of New Jerusalem in the future will be transparent.

The Gates of the City

21.12,13,21 "Having twelve gates"—According to 21.21 the street of the city is singular in number. Since there are twelve gates we would naturally assume that there should be twelve streets. Why though, is there only one street? It may possibly be that the street is like a city plaza which is open to the gates on every side.

"And at the gates, twelve angels"—The angels here are guarding the gates of the new city, not reigning over the city.

"And names written thereon, which are the names of the twelve tribes of the children of Israel"—Israel represents the law of God. "And the twelve gates were twelve pearls" (21.21)—Pearl stands for the righteousness of God. Together they show that the entry into the city of God is according to God's law and righteousness.

The Height of the City

21.14–17 "And the wall of the city had twelve foundations"—According to 21.16 an angel measures the city with a golden reed: "And the city lieth foursquare, . . . twelve thousand furlongs: the length and the breadth and the height thereof are equal" (21.16); but then it is said that "he measured the wall thereof, a hundred and forty and four cubits" (21.17). How are these calculations to be reconciled? The total height of the city is 12,000 furlongs (1500 miles), while the height of the wall is 144 cubits (72 yards). The total height is measured from the bottom foundation to the throne of God. The figure of 12,000 furlongs is a multiple of 12 which is the eternally perfect number.

The wall of the city has twelve foundations. It is quite likely that they are built one upon another and that the upper level is smaller than the lower level, similar to the structure of the Egyptian pyramid. Hence all twelve layers are visible.

"And on them twelve names of the twelve apostles of the Lamb"—The apostles represent the grace of God, therefore it is the grace of God which forms the foundations of the city wall.

City and Wall

21.18 "And the building of the wall thereof was jasper"—The city itself is of pure gold. Hence the gold is transparent, something quite different from ordinary gold.

21.19,20 "The foundations of the wall of the city were adorned with all manner of precious stones"—There are twelve precious stones with twelve various hues.

Some suggest that the colors of these precious stones are:
(1) Green, (2) Blue, (3) Blue, (4) Green, (5) Red, (6) Red,
(7) Yellow, (8) Sea-green, (9) Yellow, (10) Golden green,
(11) Purple, and (12) Purple.

The blending of these colors must be of exquisite beauty.
The merging of the colors from (5) to (12) above will
produce a rainbow-like appearance.

21.22 There is no temple in the new city. During the
Old Testament period only the temple was holy, the rest of
the land was not reckoned holy. At the time of the Lord
Jesus the temple was still on the earth. During the church
period there is a temple in heaven but none on earth. In the
millennium, however, there will be a temple on earth as
well as one in heaven. In the new heaven and the new earth
there will no more be a temple, since there will be no need
to offer sacrifice for sin. The entire new city is most holy.
Formerly, men communed with God through the temple;
now, all who live in the city can commune with God
directly because He and the Lamb have become the center
of this new city.

21.23 It is said here that there is no need for the sun
and moon to shine upon the new city. It does not say,
however, that there will be neither sun nor moon in the new
heaven and the new earth. Having the glory of God to
lighten the city and the Lamb as its lamp, the new city
certainly has no need for the sun and the moon to shine
upon it.

21.24 "And the nations shall walk amidst the light
thereof"—All who live in the city have a resurrected body,
but those who dwell on the new earth still possess a body of
flesh and blood. These are the nations dwelling on the new

earth, though they are no longer divided by race or tongue or tribe. These are the people who live at the end of the millennium and who are not deceived by Satan at the last revolt.

The saved in the city include all who believe in the Lord and trust in His precious blood—both during the Old and the New Testament times; for the gates of the new city have the names of the twelve tribes of Israel and the foundations of the city have the names of the twelve apostles.

All who live in the new city are sons (21.7), and they reign as kings (22.3). All who dwell on the new earth are those people who are transferred livingly from the millennial kingdom to be the peoples (21.3) of the new earth.

"The kings of the earth" are those who rule among the nations in eternity. They are higher in rank than the rest of the people, yet they are not the same as the kings in the city. Our Lord is the King of all kings, and we believers are kings of these kings of the earth.

"Walk" means travel. During the millennium the earthly Jerusalem will be deemed the capital of the world. The nations will travel to it once every few years. Now, in eternity, the nations will also travel to the New Jerusalem. They will be guided in their travel by the light of the city, thus they need no other guidance. (The light of the city will guide them just as the star mentioned in Matthew 2.9 guided the magi from the East.) The city itself needs no earthly light, yet the people on earth depend on the light of the city.

"And they shall bring the glory and the honor of the nations into it"—The "glory" mentioned here probably means, according to the Old Testament understanding, the best products of the lands. It is quite evident from Genesis 31 that the word "glory" there applies to property or good things on earth. In bringing their glory to the city, the nations bring in the best from their lands as offerings to God (cf. also Esther 1.4).

21.25 According to this verse there will still be night and day in the new heaven and the new earth. The kings of the earth may travel towards the new city in the daytime. In the new city, however, there is no night.

The conditions of the people in the new heaven and the new earth will be somewhat similar to the conditions of Adam and Eve before the fall. They still have a body of flesh and blood.

Five times in this book "day and night" or "night" is mentioned in connection with eternity (7.15, 14.11, 20.10, 21.25, 22.5). Therefore, there must be day and night in the new heaven and the new earth. Nevertheless, in the city there is no night, and hence the people who live there can serve God day and night. Since they have a resurrection body, they will never grow tired; thus can it be said that they are able to serve God day and night.

21.26 The peoples of the nations will follow their kings in bringing glory and honor to the city. Things work out most harmoniously.

21.27 "Anything unclean" can also be translated "anything common", which means things that are worth nothing.

"He that maketh an abomination" refers to idol-worshipers. "A lie" points especially to witchcraft and sorcery. This does not mean that there will still be idol-worship and sorcery in eternity. It only reflects upon the fact of how clean, how solemn, and how noble *is* the city.

"They that are written in the Lamb's book"—In the new heaven and the new earth dwell two kinds of people.

One kind of people are those of us who have been saved through the blood of the Lord Jesus and are privileged to live in the new city; the other kind of people are those who are removed livingly from the millennial kingdom into the new heaven and the new earth, thus becoming the inhabitants of the new earth. Our names being written in the book of life, we may permanently live in the city. The inhabitants of the new earth have their names also written in the book of life, but they can only go in and out of the new city.

The style of living of these inhabitants of the new earth is very much similar to that of Adam before the fall (except that there will not be any sinning in eternity). This view of the similarity to Adam prior to the fall is backed up by the following proofs:

(1) "In the resurrection", said the Lord, "they neither marry, nor are given in marriage" (Matt. 22.30). Only those with a resurrection body are not engaged in marriage. The inhabitants of the new earth do not have a resurrection body, therefore they will still be involved in marriage.

(2) The situation in the new heaven and the new earth is similar to that in the garden of Eden before Adam's fall. Consequently, the inhabitants of the new earth will live and multiply as Adam did of old.

(3) Of the Ten Commandments one in part says this: "Showing loving-kindness unto a thousand generations of them that love me and keep my commandments" (Ex. 20.6 mg.). If mankind does not propagate itself over a thousand generations, how can God ever make such a promise? From Adam to the Lord Jesus there were only 76 generations (Luke 3.23–38 counts God in the genealogy, thus adding up to 77 generations). The time from Adam to Christ was about 4000 years, and in such a long period there were only 76 generations! How many generations can there have been from Christ to the present? Computing scientifically and

taking 30 years as one generation, then in 2000 years there
can only be 70 to 80 generations. During the millennium
people will live long, hence there will be fewer generations.
Now granting that there might be as many as 50 generations during the millennium, the total for these three
periods will only account for 200 to 300 generations.
Subtract 300 from only a thousand, we still have 700 left.
How will these remaining generations ever be fulfilled?
Doubtless the inhabitants of the new earth will continue to
be fruitful and to multiply, except that there will be no
more death.

22.1,2 "A RIVER OF WATER OF LIFE"

22.1 This section continues to speak of the new city.
Formerly, there issued forth from the garden of Eden four
rivers; here, however, in the new city there is to be but one
river of the water of life. How much more excellent will this
be than the garden of Eden.

"The throne"—This book speaks of the throne in its
various aspects:

(1) During the gospel age God sits on the throne, and
the Lord sits with God (3.21b).

(2) During the millennial kingdom God sits on the
throne in heaven but the Lord Jesus has also a throne on
earth (3.21a).

(3) At the time of the Great White Throne the Son sits
on the Father's throne (20.11).

(4) In the new city there is but one throne—"the throne
of God and of the Lamb" (22.1). There is no more
distinction between the Father and the Son concerning the
throne.

In eternity the name of the Lord will forever be "the
Lamb", which name will forever remind men that once

there had been sin in the world but that the Lord came to the earth to be the Lamb who atoned for the sin of the world. Owing to the fact that the Lord has come as the Lamb, men are now able to eat the fruit of the tree of life and to drink of the river of the water of life.

22.2 "The tree of life" here is literal. Although in Proverbs 3.18, 11.30, 13.12, and 15.4 the tree of life is spoken of symbolically, here it cannot be interpreted in that way. For since the angel immediately explained the "many waters" mentioned in 17.15, therefore if the tree of life cited here in 22.2 is also symbolic, the angel would have instantly explained it also; but there is no explanation, and hence it is not symbolic.

Revelation 2 mentions "the tree of life, which is in the Paradise of God" (v.7). Here in 22.2 the tree of life is spoken of as being in the midst of the street (or plaza). This indicates that New Jerusalem is the Paradise of God. The garden paradise described in Genesis 2.8 is man's paradise, but this is God's paradise. God is leading men into something far better.

"The tree of life" is singular in the original. How can one tree grow on the two sides of the river, as is mentioned in this verse? There should be no problem in this matter, since a tree can send out many stems to the ground and be re-rooted.

"Yielding its fruit every month" suggests the presence of the moon. The day and the night spoken of in 21.25 is determined by the sun, but the month mentioned here is fixed by the moon. There are twelve hours in the day and twelve in the night, and also twelve months in a year. The number for eternity is twelve.

"And the leaves of the tree were for the healing of the nations"—In 12.4 it is said that there will be no more pain or death, which in addition intimates that there is no more disease. But nowhere is it stated that there will be no more weakness (see Matt. 8.17 and cf. "infirmities" with "diseases"). There is a difference between disease and weakness. Where will this weakness come from? Well, since the people on the new earth possess a body of flesh and blood, they will still be subject to weakness. How, then, can they live forever? Apparently the leaves of the tree of life must heal their weakness continuously so that they will not be wearied.

Some may ask whether it is possible for the inhabitants of the new earth to obtain eternal life. This verse does not give us a plain answer. (According to Genesis 2.9 the tree of life was definitely planted in the garden of Eden. According to our verse here, in the new heaven and the new earth the tree of life is found in the new city. But whether the nations eat of the tree of life is something unknown to us.)

22.3-5 THE SEVENFOLD GLORY OF THE REDEEMED

22.3 "And there shall be no curse any more"—This word guarantees the complete absence of sinning in the new heaven and the new earth. The tree of the knowledge of good and evil has done its work. Before Adam sinned, his conscience was not activated. In the new heaven and the new earth everyone has a conscience which can differentiate between good and evil, but the devil will not be present at that time.

Consequently, there is no curse anymore. In support of this, consider the following:

(1) The curse of the world originated as a result of the sinning of the archangel. In eternity, though, the angels are no longer in authority; we shall be placed in authority instead.

(2) Although the serpent was once used by the devil for his deceitful work, there is no mention of animals being in the new heaven and the new earth.

(3) By making wine from grapes Noah sinned and brought down a new curse upon a portion of mankind. Besides the tree of life, however, there is no record of any other plant being in the new heaven and the new earth.

"And the throne of God and of the Lamb shall be therein"—Seven times in this book the relationship between the Lord Jesus and the new city is established by the use of the name "Lamb" (21.9,14,22,23,27; 22.1,3).

"His servants" refers back to chapter 1.1. They include all the prophets and the saints of the Old Testament period as well as all of us who are saved in the New Testament era.

"Shall serve Him"—The service in view here is not one of servitude but of priestly service. It is mentioned in 20.6 that the overcomers shall be priests and kings to God. In eternity there will be no more sin, hence the priestly function is not prominently pointed out. Nevertheless, there will still be many areas wherein we can serve God. We are not supposed to pass our time idly in eternity.

In the millennial kingdom the overcomers alone will function as priests; but in eternity all the saved ones shall serve God as priests.

22.4 "And they shall see his face"—In the millennial kingdom only the overcomers shall see God's face (Heb. 12.14), since to see the face of God constantly is a special privilege. Those who perish "shall suffer punishment, even eternal destruction from the face of the Lord and from the glory of his might" (2 Thess. 1.9). In the Old Testament era Moses was only granted favor to see the back of God. In the new city, however, all the saved ones shall see God's face constantly and shall draw near to Him.

Note that 22.3 says "of God and of the Lamb" but here in 22.4 it merely says "his face", thus attesting the fact that the Son and the Father are one. They are distinguishable, but not separable.

"And his name shall be on their foreheads"—During the millennial kingdom, the 144,000 alone have His name on their foreheads (14.1). Now, though, on the foreheads of *all* the redeemed shall His name be written.

22.5 At that time there will be no need for either natural light or artificial light, because the Lord God himself shall shine upon them.

"And they shall reign for ever and ever"—To reign is the second thing to do in eternity, the first being to serve God. In the millennial kingdom only the overcomers may reign, and for a thousand years. Now, however, all who are saved shall reign, and reign forever.

Some well-known commentators suggest that 21.9–22.5 does not speak of the situation in the new heaven and the new earth, but rather describes the scene in the millennial kingdom. The reason for such interpretation is to be found in the words "the leaves of the tree were for the healing of the nations" (22.2). They argue that this verse shows that there is still disease and therefore death on earth. And hence the whole passage must refer to the millennial period. However, the following reasons will demonstrate the fallacy of such an interpretation:

(1) New Jerusalem only descends (21.2) after the old heaven and old earth are passed away (21.1). Before the old earth has passed away it is impossible for New Jerusalem to come down out of heaven from God, because it simply will not land on the old earth.

(2) 21.2 and 21.10 tell us of the New Jerusalem which comes down out of heaven from God. During the millennial

kingdom there will still be the Old Jerusalem on earth. Should the New Jerusalem descend at this time, will there not then be two Jerusalems on earth? How can the New Jerusalem descend before the Old Jerusalem has disappeared?

(3) In 21.1,2 John first saw the new heaven and the new earth, and then he saw New Jerusalem. How can anyone say that New Jerusalem in the new heaven and new earth is already there on the old earth during the millennium? Even so, some argue further that though 21.1–8 does admittedly point to the new heaven and new earth, 21.9–22.5 looks back upon the situation of New Jerusalem in the millennial kingdom. Yet do not both 21.2 and 21.10 say the same thing concerning New Jerusalem—that she comes down out of heaven from God? The New Jerusalem spoken of in 21.10 is therefore the same city as seen in 21.2.

(4) 21.5 says, "Behold, I make all things new"—How can New Jerusalem not be new but simply be the scene in the millennial kingdom before everything is made new?

(5) 21.8 describes those people who are judged after the millennial kingdom and cast into the lake of fire. Since the new city is in opposition to the lake of fire, can we at all say that this new city arrives first whereas the casting into the lake of fire of these people will occur a thousand years later?

(6) 21.22 reads: "I saw no temple therein", but we know for certain that there will be a temple during the millennium as foretold by Ezekiel (chs. 40–48).

(7) 21.23 states that "the city hath no need of the sun, neither of the moon", but we know from the Bible that during the millennium "the light of the moon shall be as the light of the sun, and the light of the sun shall be sevenfold, as the light of seven days" (Is. 30.26). How, then, can we say that New Jerusalem has descended on earth at the millennium?

(8) Both 21.24 and 21.26 speak of going "into" the city. Yet during the millennium the city is suspended in the air, with no possibility for flesh and blood to enter it.

(9) The Lamb's book of life (21.27) is seen after the millennium is over (20.15). How can people whose names are written in the Lamb's book of life go in and out of the city during the millennial kingdom?

(10) 22.3 asserts that in the new heaven and the new earth there will be no more curse. Nevertheless, in the millennium such curses as disease, pain, death, and so forth still continue. It is therefore impossible to regard 21.9–22.5 as referring to the millennial kingdom.

(11) 22.3 mentions "the throne of God and of the Lamb"—During the millennium there is only the throne of the Lord Jesus on earth, hence no mentioning of the throne of God and of the Lamb. And hence this likewise eliminates the application of 21.9–22.5 to the millennial kingdom.

(12) 22.1,2 declares that the throne of God and of the Lamb is situated in the midst of the street or plaza of the new city, whereas the prophet Ezekiel saw in his vision that the glory of the Lord filled the holy temple. If New Jerusalem descends at the millennium, where will be the center of worship—the new city or the temple on earth? Where will God dwell?

We may therefore conclude the following:

(1) that 21.9–22.5 describes the New Jerusalem,

(2) that 6.1–22.5 covers the prophetic part of this book, and

(3) that 22.6–21 does not belong to the main body of prophecy. It instead serves as an epilogue.

PART ELEVEN

THE LAST WARNING

The Last Warning
(22.6–21)

22.6 "These words" have reference to the passage given above on New Jerusalem. All that is said about New Jerusalem is faithful and true.

Twice in this book the angel declares: "These words are faithful and true" (21.5, 22.6).

"The Lord, the God of the spirits of the prophets"—The word "spirits" here is plural (cf. 1 Cor. 14.32). When the plural number of "spirit" is used it is related to spiritual gifts which edify the church.

"The spirits of the prophets" include the spirits of the prophets in both Old and New Testament times.

The words "the Lord, the God" point to the Lord Jesus. Compare 22.6 with 1.1—"He sent and signified it by his angel": In 1.1 it is said that the Lord Jesus sent His angel, and here in 22.6 the Lord God who is none other than the Lord Jesus again sends His angel (see also 22.16).

Though beginning from 22.6 we have the epilogue, it completely returns to chapter 1 of the book of Revelation.

"To show unto his servants"—This book stresses our individual responsibility before God as servants, not as children.

"The things which must shortly come to pass"—Some may consider these two thousand years to be much delay, yet the pace of things is not decided by our human concept of time but by God's sense of the hour.

22.7 "And behold, I come quickly"—Verse 6 is spoken by the angel; verse 7 is spoken by the Lord Jesus.

Three times is the sentence "Behold, I come quickly" recorded within this book's final section, 22.6–21 (vv. 7,12, and 20). This repetition is for the purpose of arousing our attention.

"Blessed is he that keepeth the words of the prophecy of this book"—This book is given to men to be kept and followed. Chapter 1.3 of the book mentions three things: read, hear, and keep. Here only "keep" is mentioned, because at this juncture people have both read and heard. What is left for us to do is to keep.

22.8 John gives a conclusion by saying that he is greatly moved by the Holy Spirit to see and to hear all the things which the Lord signified to him by the angel.

"Angel"—Probably this is the same angel as was seen in 19.10–20 and 21.9.

"I fell down to worship before the feet of the angel"— This is John's second falling down before the angel (19.10 records the first time). John had just fallen down to worship when he was immediately forbidden by the angel before he could utter any word of adoration. Hence a Christian should assume no prostrating position as a sign of worship to anyone other than to God.

22.9 God definitely forbids any worship other than to himself.

In the Old Testament era the Lord frequently appeared as an angel. In this book, He sometimes took the same angelic form. But after the millennial kingdom is over He will no longer assume the form of an angel.

22.10 clearly states that this is a book of prophecy and that it should not be sealed. Daniel 12 declares this: "Go thy way, Daniel; for the words are shut up and sealed till the time of the end" (v.9). The book of Daniel is symbolic in nature and covers a prolonged period. It was to be sealed till the end time. The book of Revelation, though, exists at the end time; therefore, it should be understood and not be sealed.

What is the meaning of being sealed? From Matthew 12.10,11,13-17 we learn that the purpose of using parables is to have the words sealed. "Seal not" used here thus shows that this book is neither parabolic nor symbolic. It is not a sealed book, but an open book.

(The error of the historical school of interpretation is to treat the entire book of Revelation symbolically. Some of the futurists in their interpretation also take a number of passages in this book symbolically. Actually this book has altogether only about twenty-eight symbols, fourteen of which are explained: such as the golden candlesticks, the seven stars, and so forth—the rest being of minor importance and easily understood. Aside from these few symbols, the contents of this book are not symbolic at all. What purpose will this book serve if most of what is in it is symbolic?)

"For the time is at hand"—Indeed, the time is very near.

22.11 We are not sure whether this word is spoken by the angel or by the Lord. This verse follows closely the preceding one. It has two meanings:

(1) Since the time is near, there will soon be no chance to turn to God if people do not return today.

(2) Within this short period, whoever is open to be transformed will be transformed, but whoever refuses to be transformed shall remain the same forever.

22.12,13 THE MESSAGE OF THE LORD

22.12 "Behold, I come quickly"—This is exactly the same as was set down in 22.7. It is said to stir up attention. This verse is connected to the preceding verse. The Lord will "render to each man according as his work is"—Let the unrighteous do unrighteousness, and the righteous do righteousness, for the Lord is coming soon.

22.13 Several times such words as these—"I am the Alpha and the Omega, the first and the last, the beginning and the end"—are proclaimed in this book (1.8 and 17, 2.8, 21.6, 22.13). The Lord persistently declares this throughout in order to impress upon us that the Old Testament Jehovah is the New Testament Jesus. God's way may change at different dispensations such as the way of the patriarchs, the way of law, and the way of grace; but God himself remains the same yesterday, today, and forever. There is only one God.

22.14-15 TWO CLASSES OF PEOPLE

22.14 This verse announces what is happening today: "Blessed are they that wash their robes"—Why blessed? For two reasons:
(1) "They may have the right to come to the tree of life"
(2) "And may enter in by the gates into the city" (This entry into the city is not to be the prerogative of the visitors, for according to 22.19 the holy city is the portion of those who have washed their robes.).

To have their robes washed is to apply the efficacy of the blood of the Lord Jesus upon them (7.14).

22.15 This passage speaks of those who perish. Let us carefully notice one thing: Do not the nations dwell outside the new city? Yes, they do. But here the "without" does not mean the new earth on which the nations dwell. By comparing 22.15 with 21.8 we can know that this place without the city is the lake of fire. As the new heaven and the new earth replace the old heaven and the old earth, as New Jerusalem supersedes Old Jerusalem, so the lake of fire in the new heaven and the new earth supplants the sea of today. Just as Topheth was outside of Jerusalem of old (2 Kings 23.10; Is. 30.33) so the lake of fire is without the new city. The use of the term "lake" implies a limited boundary.

"The dogs"—This is used symbolically. The meaning is not hard to discern. By reading Matthew 7.6 and Philippians 3.2 we can readily see that the dogs refer to those who are the unclean and who are the morally corrupt.

"And the sorcerers"—Those who communicate with demons. King Saul must die because he attempted to communicate with an evil spirit. God delivered Saul into the hand of his enemy, for God hates the spiritualists. He forbids us to consult with the dead.

22.16 CHRIST'S OWN TESTIMONY

This book is for the church. The Lord sends His angel to testify these things that His people may hear.

This verse reveals the Lord's double relationship:

(1) His relationship to the Jews and the kingdom. "I am the root . . . of David" (speaking of His divinity, David came out of Him). This suggests that He is the Jehovah of the Old Testament. As David was chosen of God to be the

first king of His own heart, so the Lord Jesus during the millennial kingdom is the King of God's own heart too. "And the offspring of David" (speaking of His humanity, the Lord Jesus came out of David). As Solomon was the son of David and was the king of peace, so the Lord Jesus in the millennial kingdom is the King of peace. These two sides answer the question raised by the Lord and recorded in Matthew 22.45: "If David then calleth him Lord, how is he his son?"

(2) His relationship with the church and with rapture. "The bright, the morning star"—Just as the morning star appears before dawn, so the Lord Jesus is the morning star to His watchful believers that they may be raptured. (The *darkest* hour is the Great Tribulation; the *dawn* is the kingdom time.)

22.17 RESPONSE OF HOLY SPIRIT AND BRIDE

The bride here is not the same as the bride mentioned in 19.7. For the bride of prophecy is concluded in 22.5. The bride here reverts to the bride mentioned in Paul's epistles— that is to say, the totality of the church is in view here (see our discussion on 19.7).

"And the Spirit and the bride say, Come"—This is the prayer of the Holy Spirit and the church. Since 22.16 is addressed especially to the church, then what is here in 22.17 is the reply.

"And he that heareth"—Such words are repeated in 1.3, 13.9 and many more times in chapters 2 and 3. Each person must hear for himself.

"And he that is athirst, let him come"—This again returns to the circumstances of the church. "Athirst" means thirsty in soul. "Come" is the same as is stated in Matthew 11.28. The words "take the water of life freely" refer not to the water of life spoken in 22.1 but allude to that eternal life which the believer receives and which enables him to be fully satisfied in Christ without thirsting after the world anymore.

Whoever longs for the soon return of the Lord will also yearn for the souls of men. He will ask for the Lord's coming on the one hand, and aspire for the salvation of the sinners on the other.

22.18-19 THE FINAL WARNING

The tree of life and the holy city are the same here as are spoken of in 22.14. The difference, however, lies in the fact that whereas 22.14 mentions only entering the holy city, 22.18 speaks about having the holy city as one's portion.

None is allowed to add to or to take away from the words of this book. The warning against this is most serious.

22.20-21 FINAL MESSAGE, PRAYER, AND BLESSING

22.20 The Lord Jesus himself testifies: "Yea: I come quickly."

"Amen: come, Lord Jesus"—This is the prayer of John. We need not ask what theory one holds concerning the second coming of the Lord; we only need to inquire whether one's heart yearns for the Lord's return and whether he seems to be a person waiting for the return of the Lord. The last prayer in the Bible is "Come, Lord Jesus"—One day this prayer will be answered. During these two thousand years many faithful believers have prayed this prayer constantly.

22.21 This is a benediction given by John. Without

"the grace of the Lord Jesus" no sinner can be saved, neither can any saint stand. The grace of the Lord Jesus alone empowers us to be raptured and to enter the kingdom.

TITLES YOU
WILL WANT TO HAVE

by Watchman Nee

Basic Lesson Series
Volume 1—A Living Sacrifice
Volume 2—The Good Confession
Volume 3—Assembling Together
Volume 4—Not I, But Christ
Volume 5—Do All to the Glory of God
Volume 6—Love One Another

The Church and the Work
Volume 1—Assembly Life
Volume 2—Rethinking the Work
Volume 3—Church Affairs

The Life That Wins
From Glory to Glory
The Spirit of Judgment
From Faith to Faith
The Lord My Portion
Aids to "Revelation"
Grace for Grace
The Better Covenant
A Balanced Christian Life
The Mystery of Creation
The Messenger of the Cross
Full of Grace and Truth—Volume 1
Full of Grace and Truth—Volume 2
The Spirit of Wisdom and Revelation
Whom Shall I Send?
The Testimony of God
The Salvation of the Soul
The King and the Kingdom of Heaven
The Body of Christ: A Reality
Let Us Pray
God's Plan and the Overcomers
The Glory of His Life
"Come, Lord Jesus"
Practical Issues of This Life
Gospel Dialogue
God's Work
Ye Search the Scriptures
The Prayer Ministry of the Church
Christ the Sum of All Spiritual Things
Spiritual Knowledge
The Latent Power of the Soul
Spiritual Authority
The Ministry of God's Word
Spiritual Reality or Obsession
The Spiritual Man

by Stephen Kaung

Discipled to Christ
The Splendor of His Ways
Seeing the Lord's End in Job
The Songs of Degrees
Meditations on Fifteen Psalms

ORDER FROM:

Christian Fellowship Publishers, Inc.
11515 Allecingie Parkway
Richmond, Virginia 23235